I think many of us who read management and leadership literature agree that this basically simple subject is slowly choking on an over indulgence of jargon, theory, models and metaphors. Yet what the practitioner wants is hands on pearls of wisdom that confirm current action and stimulate new ideas. All great teachers and leaders down through the ages have done this successfully by telling real life stories to get the point across. So it is with this publication by Doctor Irv Rubin. He is a man who travels the world to demystify the subject of management for thousands and this publication is about those travels and the stories of those who have benefited from the practical wisdom of this great human being.

—Reg Garters CEO New Zealand Institute of Management Canterbury Author of <u>Time to Manage Time—a prescription for personal and corporate effectiveness</u> and <u>Managing to Lead—reality v rhetoric</u>

Irv Rubin is world class when it comes to combining rigorous theoretical thinking with heart-felt, experience-based wisdom. I doubt you'll have the patience to read only one of these 52 stimulating essays per week for a year. I couldn't put the book down once I started reading it. Now I'm going back and reviewing and studying one per week in the context of each the others. During my career I've encountered only a few true thought leaders in the field of organizational leadership—Irv Rubin is one. Curbside Consulting is the best vehicle you'll ever find for picking the brain, heart and soul of a true genius.

—Dick Lyles, Best selling author and independent international consultant.

CURBSIDE
CONSULTING

CURBSIDE CONSULTING

Irwin M. Rubin Ph.D.

iUniverse, Inc.

New York Lincoln Shanghai

CURBSIDE CONSULTING

iUniverse books may be ordered through booksellers or by contacting:

iUniverse
2021 Pine Lake Road, Suite 100
Lincoln, NE 68512
www.iuniverse.com
1-800-Authors (1-800-288-4677)

The information, ideas, and suggestions in this book are not intended as a substitute for professional advice. Before following any suggestions contained in this book, you should consult your personal physician or mental health professional. Neither the author nor the publisher shall be liable or responsible for any loss or damage allegedly arising as a consequence of your use or application of any information or suggestions in this book.

ISBN-13: 978-0-595-41202-0 (pbk)
ISBN-13: 978-0-595-85558-2 (ebk)
ISBN-10: 0-595-41202-5 (pbk)
ISBN-10: 0-595-85558-X (ebk)

Printed in the United States of America

Contents

Preface

Well-worn phrases like curbside consulting and water cooler wisdom all point to the same simple truth. When people take a few moments to share their experience strength and hope with one another, the result is something 'broader, smarter, wiser' than either one had before. Each one has more wisdom and advice to apply to their own professional and personal life challenges, and to pass on to others.

Over my lifetime friends, colleagues, clients, and significant others have generously shared their experience and wisdom with me. Sometimes I received it with an open mind and heart and my life was better as a result. Other times, for seemingly very rational reasons at the time I discounted it…only to see its wisdom and value after a few more painful learning experiences. Upon still other occasions, equally painful experience taught me that someone else's truth might not be mine. Consequently, the advice spawned by our experience and the wisdom, which fuels our strength and hope, have in common an important fact: both are the result of relationships with others and are passed on via relationships with others.

<u>Curbside Consulting</u>, therefore, can best be viewed as a point along a relational continuum. It reflects the cumulative result of gifts that others have given me. You will relate to the content and images contained in your own unique way. You will create a new perspective, based on who you are. When you next have a 'passing conversation'—be it by the curbside or the water cooler—you can relate the experience strength and hope any specific essay 'gifted' to you. In other words, if it seems appropriate, share your reflections, conclusions, and reactions about what you read with a friend, colleague, client and or significant other.

Each of the fifty-two essays is keep short—600-800 words. Curbside consultations are equally brief encounters. As a result, the I.Q. portions of our left-brains will not hopefully, become overwhelmed with abstractions. The graphic images that accompany each essay are intended to 'speak' to our right brains. This is where the wisdom of our Emotional Intelligence—our E.Q.—is rooted. Finally, essay titles [See Table of Contents] have been carefully chosen to reflect words often used in the start of a curbside encounter: "Have you got a minute? I've been wondering about 'XXXX.'"

Continuous efforts to find the "one right way" to sequence each of the essays resulted only in frustration. Today's rational framework yielded to tomorrow's better idea. Consequently, the essays appear in the order in which they were 'birthed.' You can, therefore, read them in any order. Let your intuition and spirit lead you to whatever curbside feels right at any given moment.

And please feel free specifically to share reflections, conclusions, and reactions about what you read with us at <u>*temenos@lava.net*</u> *so we can help to **anonymously** pass them along to others.*

In this way continuing 'curbside consultations' will become win-win conversations mixing together unique individual perspectives, leaving each of us potentially 'broader, smarter, wiser' as a result.

Acknowledgments

Keeping with the spirit of 'curbside consultations' the acknowledgements section will be equally brief. As has been noted: "Over my lifetime friends, colleagues, clients, and significant others have generously shared their experience and wisdom with me." I extend my sincerest thanks to all of them—those that I can recall and those who have faded in my 'senior moments!'

A picture, as we all know, is often worth a thousand words. The artworks that accompany each curbside consultation are the creative contributions of Dave Swann, Bryant Fukutomi, and Kip Aoki and are used with the kind permission of the Honolulu Star-Bulletin and to acknowledge Jaime Ubongen for his creative efforts as well.

Finally, the painstaking process of preparing the final manuscript was carried to completion by my Temenos colleague Doreen Gurtiza, with 'curbside consultations' as needed from Tracy Ubongen, who manages somehow to manage both of us, as well as the Temenos office. Thank you both very much.

Week 1
Creating Excellence Requires Hard Accounting For The Soft Stuff

Illustrated by Jaime Ubongen

Did you ever run into a business professing, "Our people are our least important asset"? Of course not! The words on plaques and posters, if they exist, always say the opposite. But businesses do not always "walk the talk."

Against all logic—given that they need more from their most important asset under times of stress and downsizing—the first budget cut when sales and profits begin to drop is, you guessed it, the training and development budget!

Underlying these actions is an unspoken, erroneous and very expensive myth: The soft-stuff of management (like leadership development, interpersonal skill building, conflict resolution and the like) have no direct bearing on the organization's hard bottom lines.

Rather, training and development are treated as a luxury.

"When we have the time and money, we will let our people off from their real work to take that 'touchy-feely stuff.'"

Let's take a hard look at the danger of this myth.

Consider the following "hypothetical example" of an organization of about 1,000 employees. Consider an average week in that organization where the following sampling of human dynamics are taking place: One person is complaining about someone to a third party who is nowhere near to hear their feedback (a game I call the triangle game); people are asking one another what the boss meant during this morning's staff meeting, rather than asking the boss directly during the meeting; a person is going around another person to get a job done because they can't get along.

A very conservative estimate of the amount of time and energy "invested" in situations like these—and they are but a small sampling of dynamics that fall into the familiar category of "office politics"—would be one half-hour per employee per week. But this very conservative figure must be at least doubled. Why?

Because every such conversation takes two people. In other words, it takes two people to have one dysfunctional interpersonal relationship.

So, the organization has now wasted 1,000 person hours that week. Multiply that figure by 50 weeks (assuming the average person gets 2 weeks vacation) and you now have 50,000 person-hours wasted.

If we next assume that an average investment per hour per employee for all employees from the CEO on down is $20 per employee hour (including wages, benefits, etc.), we have accounted for, conservatively, $1 million directly off of the bottom line. Double the original conservative estimate of one half-hour per employee per week and you will account for $2 million directly off the bottom line.

Still think the "touchy-feely stuff" is a luxury?

Week 2
Are You Talking To Me?
Avoiding Conflict Can Be Dangerous

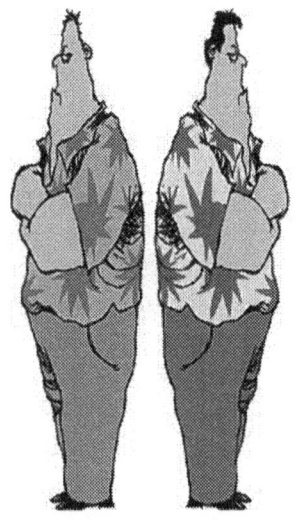

Illustrated by David Swann

It's sad to say that the terms "conflict" and "confrontation" make some people very uncomfortable. Many people dislike conflict so much they will go to great lengths to avoid it. They'll postpone regular medical check-ups, for example, even though there's a strong history of cancer in their families. It's as if they believe that the examination itself will cause the disease to appear.

With organizations, conflict avoidance can take a variety of forms. These range from the passive, taking a deep breath and ducking one's head; to more active forms like placating, "It's just a semantic difference! We're really saying the same thing", to putting off the issue, "We need more data before we can decide. Let's table it." or to pulling rank, "We've discussed this enough. We'll do X."

Autocratic leaders, like managers who deal with conflicts by pulling rank, will often actually, themselves, generate very high levels of interpersonal tension that gets hidden behind forced smiles. In the apparent absence of conflict that follows, what is really apathy then gets classified as team harmony.

After reviewing hours of videotaped senior management team meetings, I've discovered that sometimes these avoidance strategies can get pretty subtle. The next time you're in a meeting and the "heat goes up" even a little bit, watch what happens.

Notice how many qualifiers you begin to hear. Watch the word "I" virtually disappear, replaced by the universal and far safer word, "We."

Listen for tentative questions as they replace declarative statements like, "Maybe we might want to do….."; "Do you think maybe we should do…"; "Perhaps if we were willing to look at it this way…" And listen carefully to humor as it arises, with its hidden double meanings.

Remember your high school days in the chemistry lab? If you took the Bunsen burner off the heat too quickly, you might miss the catalytic reaction; if you left it on too long, the vial would crack. We face the same challenge in effective conflict management. Sensitivity to timing and the skills to discern the shifting of consequences are qualities that can and must be learned and practiced.

Consider, too, that confrontation has its roots in the Latin term, frons, meaning the forehead. So, confrontation really means, "putting our foreheads together." (Remember the old adage, "Two heads are better than one"?)

When two stags are "butting heads" in the forest, their purpose is not really to harm each other; they're actually collaborating by helping each other get "sharper." Their "play" makes them better prepared to beat off their natural enemies. Effective and constructive confrontation in an organization can also result in sharper ideas, the kind needed to stay ahead of the competition.

Avoiding conflict not only prolongs a problem, it causes it to get worse, and, along the way, prevents the discovery of many creative opportunities. That's a lose-lose "dis-ease" that organizations in search of excellence can ill afford.

Week 3
Leading To Points Unknown

Illustrated by Kip Aoki

The search for excellence can take one of two general paths.

The first is to do everything possible to perfect and refine an already known process or tool. Like an Olympic athlete who strives in every way possible to reduce their performance time by hundredths of seconds, the objective is to beat the competition by following an already well-beaten path and doing it better.

The second strategy involves leaving the beaten path altogether. Its objective is to gain an edge on the competition by creating a new product or service before someone else does.

The critical distinction between these two paths in terms of their impact on leadership can be understood by reflecting back to the challenges Columbus faced in 1492.

In the early part of his voyage to the New Land, his leadership skills were primarily those of a map-*reader;* the seas he journeyed upon had already been charted. However, Columbus soon came to the point where the navigators who had come before him had chosen to turn back in the face of uncertainty and ambiguity. There were no beaten paths, no charts. From then on, Columbus's leadership relied on his ability to be a map*maker*.

One of the things he did was to place a trusted man at the ship's bow. At the same time that this man was on the lookout for unknown reefs, he would take frequent depth soundings and call them back to the bridge. Using this constant stream of communication, Columbus was able to create a new map, one that others would eventually follow as they beat their own path to the New Lands.

During periods of intense uncertainty, it's often been my experience to witness that leaders will bury themselves in the "safety" of their offices.

Why do they do this? Well, who among us relishes the looks and stares that mapmakers get from their fearful crews who aren't sure where their leaders are taking them? Particularly when the most honest answer they could give might be "No, I'm not sure exactly where we're going, but I have faith we're on the right track. If we stay focused, keep supporting each other and not waste our energies in rebellion we will come through this even stronger."

There's an old Sufi saying that captures the essence of this leadership challenge well: "I never taught anyone archery who at some point did aim their arrows at my back."

In other words, organization leaders who seeks to leave the beaten path in order to find a "new land" of truly innovative solutions and products, must be prepared to cope with considerable emotional turmoil from their crews. And any such leader must possess a unique set of communication skills to ensure that this turmoil—which is entirely natural—doesn't erupt into a full-blown mutiny. Because in organizations, as on ships, the first people to jump to seek other jobs are the strongest swimmers. It's guaranteed that if you allow your competition to steal away your best people, you cannot beat them.

Especially in times of uncertainty, it's imperative that leaders evolve from being map-readers to mapmakers and this can be done using learnable skills.

But true vision also requires that leaders must reach deep inside themselves for two qualities no amount of training can give—courage and faith.

Week 4
Is This Your Boss?

Illustrated by Bryant Fukutomi

"Houston, we have a problem."

When that famous sentence echoed from the space ship to NASA headquarters in Houston, a well oiled, highly trained, committed group of skilled professionals focused on a singular objective. Office politics were forgotten. Anxieties about political correctness were minimal. Any and every idea that could help was voiced, considered, and chewed apart—regardless of its hierarchical source.

Consider, by contrast, the current and persistent following patterns of behavior that characterize corporate organizational dynamics by asking yourself the following question. [Adapted from "The Practice of Empowerment", by Dennis Kinslow.] You can be fully honest since no one but you will "hear" your response.

1. If you knew that a supervisor in your organization was doing something that was hurting the organization, would you confront that person?

2. Do you know of some way that your organization could make a substantial gain in cutting its costs or improving the quality of its goods and services?

3. And will you do anything about it?

When several thousand people, just like yourself, were asked these questions, the pattern of responses to the three questions was as follows: (1) Less than 50 percent said yes. (2) Almost 100 percent said yes. (3) Less than 10 percent said yes. If you're the chief executive of a large corporation (or even a small one), these data should stop you dead in your tracks. Their implications are immediate and clear.

For example, questions No. 2 & No.3 above confirm that there is a veritable gold mine of underused creative potential just waiting to be released among your people. That's the good news. The bad news is that traditional suggestion boxes will not release this potential.

The key factor that will do so is being certain that all of your supervisors are skilled in creating environments where employees feel encouraged, safe, and appreciated for bringing forth any and all ideas. Regardless of their hierarchical source. And, specifically those ideas that might have to do with how a supervisor's own behavior might be "the something that was hurting the organization."

This point brings is face-to-face with the implications of question No.1 above. It tells us, in no uncertain terms, that as a CEO, there is a greater than 50 percent probability that your own reports would not tell you directly if you were doing something they thought was potentially hurting the organization.

And, lest we forget, your behavior and your decisions are expected to have a huge impact on the organization. That's the bad news.

The really bad news is that the current craze of hiding behind anonymous averaged 360-degree feedback mechanisms will only serve to make the underlying problem worse.

Why worse and not better? Because such feedback mechanisms not only do nothing to help people learn to communicate face-to-face, they actually reinforce not doing so. Under the guise of "People wouldn't be honest otherwise!" we continue not to help people learn how to communicate wisely, honestly, and compassionately, face-to-face.

As the senior "supervisor" who sets the standard for others to follow, ask yourself a few hard questions.

What do you do to make it safe for your people to give you direct face-to-face feedback? How much do they really trust you to be open-minded and non-defensive? How open are you to some of the "cost cutting and improving the quality of your goods and services ideas" that virtually 100 percent of them have? And, most importantly, how do you know your own responses to these hard questions are really valid?

We most certainly have a problem. Its roots and implications spread far and wide, well beyond Houston. We seem not to have learned from the oft-quoted truth voiced by the prison guard in the movie "Cool Hand Luke" when he said, "What we have here is a failure to communicate."

Rather, what we continue to have is a failure to do anything substantive about our failure to communicate.

Week 5
Finding Garcia: Lessons For The Rest Of Us

Illustrated by David Swann

[Note: Over 100 years ago, a newspaper reporter named Elbert Hubbard wrote an article he intended to be filler for some empty space. The essence of that article and its current relevance to all of us follows below.]

When the war broke out between Spain and the United States, President McKinley knew he had to communicate quickly with Garcia, the leader of the insurgents. The problem was that Garcia was holed up—out of reach by any mail or telegraph—somewhere in the mountains of Cuba. Without Garcia's cooperation, many lives would be needlessly lost. A nondescript and unremarkably average man by the name of Andrew Rowan was given the task of delivering the letter. Upon being handed the letter sealed in an oilskin pouch by McKinley, Rowan was simply told; "Deliver this to Garcia personally as quickly as possible." Rowan said absolutely nothing, saluted, did an about face, and left the President's Office.

The highlights of Rowan's journey are as follows: Four days later he jumped out of an open boat in the middle of the night off the coast of Cuba and disappeared, alone, into the thick jungle. Three weeks later, having successfully traversed a hostile country on foot he re-emerged on the other side having fulfilled his mission.

Compare that scenario with what might happen if you asked one of your rank-and-file employees, chosen completely at random, to do 'something important as quickly as possible'. Would that person have acted like Rowan? Or would the person have asked you for a more detailed explanation as to why, about how this task fit into other priorities, what quickly as possible really meant? Would the person have sought information as to 'Garcia's last known location'? Might you have gotten a 'stink eye' look that said; 'It ain't in my job description.' How likely is it that the person to whom you delegated the responsibility would seek to 'pass the buck' along to someone else?

There are Rowan's out there. We see one every now and again. But we more often see their opposites—people who procrastinate, blame, make excuses and shrink away from accountability. Who will do anything to avoid following the Nike challenge and 'Just do it.' So the challenge is to identify a few simple principles we can we learn from President McKinley's behavior as the "CEO" in this story to increase the number of Rowan's in our own organizations?

McKinley began with a very specific measurable stretch goal, one clearly linked to the military mission of the organization: "Deliver this to Garcia personally as quickly as possible." There could be no question in Rowan's mind of the urgency and importance of a message "sealed in an oilskin pouch."

Along with a specific mission-related goal, McKinley communicated the clearest expectations possible under the circumstances; deliver it "personally" and "as quickly as possible." Some would argue that the latter point is too ambiguous. However, given the fact that no one knew where in Cuba Garcia was holed up, any more specificity would have eroded McKinley's credibility as a leader giving an assignment. Expectations have to be clear and reasonable to be motivating of excellence.

McKinley never once communicated the slightest doubt that Rowan would succeed. He allowed the self-fulfilling power of the Pygmalion Effect—people will strive their very best to do what you, in your heart, believe is the very best they can do—to do its work.

Finally, and this is perhaps the hardest lesson to take from this story. Having done all that he could himself do, President McKinley had to trust Rowan to do his best. No micro managing. No requirements for frequent up-dates or lengthy written reports, which could have distracted Rowan from his singular task.

In the midst of all the rational techniques upon which managers must rely—budgets, 5-year plans, etc.—there may be an even more important message in Rowan's story. Trust may be the hidden factor determining an employee's willingness to go the extra yard that is always associated with the pursuit of excellence.

Week 6
One Size Doesn't Fit All

Illustrated by Honolulu Star-Bulletin Staff

Two friends, senior managers from different corporations in town, are having their weekly lunch together. One says, with obvious enthusiasm and excitement, "I can't wait to tell you about the incredible team-building session we had this last weekend!" The other responds with equally intense feelings, but his reflect chagrin and frustration. "We had a session too. And what a waste of time it was!"

There are many factors that can cause such vastly different reactions. But in my experience, what is central among them is the false belief that "one size fits all" when it comes to methods of team building. And this belief is common to both consultants and clients alike.

Let's look at sports as an analogy of what I mean. A baseball team is a group that requires minimal connectedness between its players in order to accomplish its task. At any one instant during a typical game, only two people are actively involved in helping the team succeed, such as the pitcher and the catcher, or the third baseman and the first baseman. A baseball team, therefore, is essentially made up of several smaller two-person components that interact with each other to carry the action forward. So in a "perfect game" of 27 strikeouts, it's conceivable that seven of the nine team members will be "standing around" watching and cheering on their star pitcher and catcher, without ever having to touch the ball themselves.

In contrast, a football team demonstrates moderate connectedness. During the huddle, the quarterback calls a certain play that will determine each of the other team members' specific jobs. If all the offensive players do their jobs perfectly, every play is "theoretically" designed to score a touchdown; and, "theoretically", if all the defensive players do their jobs perfectly, the offense will never gain a single yard. Consequently, some players, such as the blocking tackles, will occasionally get to score a touchdown, but only if someone else makes a mistake, like "dropping the ball."

At the other end of the spectrum, a basketball team's members are very connected. If the players "stand around" watching their star players, the team is guaranteed to lose. To win at basketball, every player has to be actively involved all the time. And unlike a football team that holds a huddle preceding most every play, a basketball coach calls for a huddle only if the situation is especially tense.

The point is, each of these teams requires a very different strategy for team building. In baseball, pairs of players, like pitchers and catchers, or in-fielders and out-fielders, can benefit from practicing together. In basketball, the entire team needs to practice together.

Effective organizational team building, too, must begin with an analysis of the nature of the work to be done—the reason for the team in the first place—and this will determine the style of building cohesiveness that's most appropriate. One size will *not* fit all.

Week 7
Without Effective Communication, There Is No Team

Illustrated by Kip Aoki

All decision-making is a form of communication. In the business world, as in the sports world, working teams need to know how they can best communicate, and this is determined by the kind of purpose the team is put together to achieve.

If the team tries to communicate like a baseball team—in a series of interactions that take place between various two-person groups within the larger whole—but the structure of the group is more like that of a basketball team—in which all the players work together—their meetings will not be productive. The final outcome, even after multiple sessions, is likely to resemble a camel, an animal described as "a horse put together by a committee."

If we were to draw a picture of the normal lines of communication on a baseball team, it might look like a series of spokes on a wheel: the pitcher throws to the catcher; a shortstop throws to a first baseman. Occasionally, three players are involved, such as when an outfielder throws to a cut-off man, who then relays it to the catcher. By contrast, the pattern of the communications between members of a basketball team would look more like a spider web. Each player must rapidly throw the ball around to someone else, the whole group looking for the player with the easiest open shot for the hoop. If these two different types of teams were both made to communicate and make decisions using only one of these patterns, one would be a sure loser.

Imagine, now, three different phases in one team meeting. In the beginning of the meeting the leader informs everyone about a decision that's already been made. The most appropriate pattern of communication at this point might look most like a baseball team's style—a series of one-to-one interactions. "Here's what I've decided about this project. Mary, you do Y. Peter, you do Z." Everyone listens carefully and makes sure they know what they're expected to do.

Next there might be a consulting process that looks like a football team's huddle. Peter says, "I have to do something about Problem A. What are all your thoughts?" Team members then "talk to the chair," giving their suggestions. If all goes well, the discussion will be spirited, with full participation from all team members, but there is little if any debate. And this is vitally important. After the "huddle" it is still the "quarterback's" responsibility to make the final decision and then to inform everyone of their part in implementing it.

Finally, there will be times when the team needs to make a true consensus decision. To start off the process, the leader might say something like, "Look, here's the situation with X. This is so important, and its implementation will involve us all, so I want us to reach a consensus."

Several things are vital—and badly misunderstood—about consensus.

First, the appropriate communication pattern would look just like the "spider web" of a basketball team, in which every member has equal chance to talk directly to everyone else, without having first to go through the chair as a mediator.

Second, and this is most difficult for managers and leaders to accept, is the fact that in a true consensus discussion there is no hierarchy. Each person's ideas are as good as everyone else's. A test of this pattern of communication is that if the consensus decision is never different from the one the leader would make by herself, true consensus has not taken place. A consensus decision means that each person's points are fully heard and given sincere consideration, regardless of the formal role each plays on the team.

Third, consensus is not the same as unanimity, or perfect agreement. Once the full discussion of different points of view has been had, the team must agree that they can and will put their full weight behind supporting and implementing the team's consensus decision.

The next time you as a team leader or team member are frustrated to see that your meeting has once again taken a horse and made a camel out of it, ask yourself these questions:

- Were you and your teammates clear as to what communication process best fit each part of the meeting?

- Were you really willing to let the outcome be a true consensus, or did it have to turn out your way?

- If your honest answer to these questions is "No," then you yourself have contributed to a bumpy ride instead of a smooth one!

Week 8
Learning How To Become A 'Good' Team Player

Illustrated by David Swann

Picture the following scenario. You're Mary Smith and you've just joined the senior management team as one of the vice presidents. This is your first team meeting. You're getting ready to sit beside Peter, one of your peers and colleagues. Peter leans over slightly and whispers, "Mary, that's George's seat. Take the next one." You feel grateful to have just barely sidestepped group protocol.

In the middle of the meeting, Sally, the CEO, interrupts George in mid-sentence and says, "No, I think the best way to handle X is to do Y."

Without even thinking, you pipe up, "Excuse me, Sally. Were you finished with your point, George?" Even without any training in group dynamics, you know what the slight gasp, raised eyebrows, and uncomfortable shifting around in seats means: you've crossed the line by stepping on an unwritten group norm.

If Peter is a real friend, he'll approach you after the meeting and give you a "Dutch Uncle" talk: "Mary, that was a land mine you just stepped on. We don't comment on Sally's running of the meeting, especially in the meeting. It could be a career—limiting move." As the new kid on the block, you are becoming socialized to the "way we do things around here."

All teams have norms, unwritten rules that significantly impact their ability to function. The vital point is this: Do the norms support or detract from the team's performance? Do they fit the team's goal or not?

Norms—*with one exception*—are inherently neither good nor bad.

For example, I've seen team meetings among 40 department heads held around a table that was 60 feet long and 5 feet wide. How much real communication and interaction would you expect between two groups of people lined up and down a bowling alley lane?

On the other hand, many years ago I had the opportunity to observe an Israeli Command unit planning a raid against an enemy location in the desert. I had had several years' prior experience consulting with the US Navy. While I didn't know what all the stripes on the Israeli soldier's uniform meant, I knew enough about what some of them did mean.

You can imagine my shock, then, when I observed the no-holds barred, heated, and emotional debate over the best plan of attack that followed. Every idea that was raised got intense feedback, face-to-face comment and scrutiny, irrespective of the rank of the person who suggested it.

This was a far cry from anything I had ever seen before in the United States, either in the military or the business world. (However, I have since witnessed several comparable examples with senior management teams who care enough about their level of teamwork to send me videos of their regular meetings. As their behavioral coach, I review these tapes and give them feedback.) In brief, I was told that when it came to planning a raid, it was considered vital that the decision be a true consensus. No idea could go unexpressed and unexplored. No matter how crazy it sounded. No matter who had the idea. When it came to consensus, rank was inconsequential. Once the plan was agreed upon, however, the established hierarchy kicked back in. In other words, implementation followed the chain of command: a different set of rules for a different set of tasks and goals.

So what's the one exception referred to earlier in this article? In an effort to avoid all conflict many teams have a rule that says, "Around here we don't openly examine and talk about our norms." A team driven by this rule will be spending an enormous amount of time and energy tiptoeing around land mines like the one Mary encountered earlier, leaving less energy and creativity available for vital consensus decisions.

Week 9
Picking Your Path

Illustrated by David Swann

When speaking recently about integrity in business and government, a respected local senior executive said, "It's harder to find than gold!" "It's more like mining for Australian fire opals!" I responded quickly. In explaining why, I commented that when you happen upon a nugget of gold, you could see its sparkle quickly. On the other hand, fire opals are generally found caked in a very thick layer of hard mud, so their brilliance is not as easy to see with the naked eye. In fact, the opal can be missed entirely if the layer of mud is not broken through.

Sadly, finding integrity in business and government these days is more like mining opals than gold. Thick layers of mud cover true quality. This mud is comprised of a variety of lies we tell ourselves to justify not doing what we know in our hearts is the right thing.

Enron's CEO and senior leadership must be taken to task and held accountable for their unethical acts, both of commission and omission that have ruined the financial lives of tens of thousands of hard-working families. But, make no mistake about it; those who are made to pay did not act alone. There were an untold number of co-conspirators within the corporations of Enron and Arthur

Anderson who chose to remain silent and bury their heads in the sand; just as there were in Watergate, just as there were in using 'weapons of mass destruction,' as justification for going to war against Iraq, and just as there were in the Bay of Pigs crisis. In the last case, we have documented evidence that trusted members of President Kennedy's cabinet willfully withheld facts because they didn't want to say things they thought the boss didn't want to hear. In that case, "groupthink" almost cost us more than several hundred million dollars. In the Bay of Pigs, the results could have been catastrophic because the boss had his hand on a 'little red button.'

As concerning and, indeed, frightening as this dynamic of silent collusion is, the justification for the behavior is even more disconcerting. When local fiascos become visible—like the Aloha Stadium rotting or a 10-year, multimillion dollar overrun of a building project at the University of Hawaii—the phrase we most often hear, accompanied by a helpless shrug of shoulders, is "That's just politics." We also hear a similar phrase when fiascos like Enron become visible, again accompanied by a helpless shrug of shoulders. "That's just business."

In contributing to and tolerating a society driven by two separate sets of ethical standards—one set for our businesses or public servants, and one set for ourselves—we have colluded in creating a very dangerous situation, most importantly for our children. In those precious few years when they are young and still at home, we struggle to teach them values like honesty, trustworthiness, courage, and integrity.

Then we send them into careers in organizations—organizations we have helped to create, manage, and lead—where they will spend over one-third of their waking hours for most of their adult lives. And in these environments—again, environments we have created for them—we are teaching them that while the IRS frowns on keeping two different sets of financial accounting records, keeping two sets of ethical accounting standards is in fact the way things are.

If we continue to allow this gap in our concept of integrity to exist between our personal and business or political ethics, there will be neither lodes of gold nor of fire opals for our children to enjoy. Instead, we will leave them a legacy of spiritual and financial bankruptcies.

For in the business of living, we are all CEOs accountable for our actions and choices. It's up to us to make choices that are commensurate with both our dreams of personal fulfillment and our sense of what is right for all of us in public life.

Week 10
Whipping Up Your Potential

Illustrated by David Swann

Even a cursory reading of Jim Collins' recent bestseller, "*Good to Great*" would be an eye-opener for many managers and leaders. It would drive home the point that the challenge facing organizations—both public and private—is counter to the old adage of having too many chiefs and not enough Indians to do a job. The real challenge is that too many "chiefs," leaders who should have what it takes to release the fullest potential of the highly motivated "Indians," don't always do what it takes to release their own fullest potential as a pre-requisite to helping others release theirs.

In the first place, great leaders recognize that their hierarchical position—be it CEO, parent, teacher, or governor—is the *least useful* means of influence at their disposal. The practice of pulling rank, either verbally or silently, with a menacing eye, will get you compliance but it will not get you real commitment.

Worse, if you continually pull rank to get people to follow your lead, you're guaranteed to kill the very creativity that your organization must have these days to survive and keep growing.

In Hawaii, for example, a plantation mentality is sadly still alive and well in many organizations. It's more subtly expressed than the "The boss will tell me what he wants me to do!" excuse for a lack of initiative heard in old days, but none-the-less debilitating.

Second, great leaders recognize that leadership is a quality that characterizes a *relationship*. Heads of corporations and business enterprises worldwide invest enormous amounts of time and money in the training and development of their future management.

And even when the going gets rough financially, they don't allow this investment to be slashed. By honing everyone's skills of collaborative conflict-resolution—beginning with their own—they are ensuring that the whole will be greater than the sum of its parts. This is particularly true in the face of the current trend of downsizing, which results in having fewer parts to handle the same workload.

Finally, no matter what their hierarchical position, great leaders are humble, not only in the office but in their personal life. They recognize and embrace the fact that being a good human being and being a good leader are one and the same.

For example, when Max Dupree was the chairman and chief executive officer for the officer furnishings leader Herman Miller Corp. he would ask for a moment of silence before he and his executive team had to make an important decision. Why? He needed to pray for the courage to put his ego aside and do the right thing for the whole. He is a man who understands that the role of a leader is as a servant to a higher calling.

Week 11
Making Your Wave

Illustrated by Bryant Fukutomi

At the peak of his career as Chief Executive Officer of General Electric, Jack Welsh was asked what it was about GE's strategic planning process that allowed the company to be so successful. The essence of his response was that in these times of rapid change and uncertainty, "predicting was less important than reacting." Let's explore this apparently simple notion.

All strategic planning models are based on the same fundamental premise: setting a plan for the future is the best way to manage uncertainty. The two key questions being addressed by strategic planning, therefore, are: "What will the future bring? and "How can we best position ourselves to make the most of the opportunities it presents?" These questions are not unlike the same ones that accomplished surfers ask themselves as they sit on their boards looking out at the ocean, getting ready for the next set of waves building on the horizon.

But suppose these two questions were re-framed to read: "What do we *want* our future to bring us? and "How can we be proactive in creating our own future?" Or, in the surfing analogy, "What can we do to make our own waves?"

Although a typical strategic plan is subject to periodic revisions, once set, it becomes the script an organization strives to follow strictly. People are measured by their ability to act out their parts, the closer to the letter the better.

So new, truly innovative ideas, which are central to continuously proactive strategic thinking, are often viewed as problems in a traditionally reactive strategic planning process. In proactive plans, "making waves" is the key to success; while in reactive plans, "waves" are seen as diversions.

Rosabeth Moss Kanter makes a similar point in the Winter 2002 MIT Sloan Management Review. The key to staying ahead of your competition, she argues, is to adopt improvisational theater as a metaphor for organizational planning. "Improvisational" does not mean random. It does mean having a clear, agreed-upon theme—or, in the case of an organization, a simple value-driven mission—and a set of attitudes and skills antithetical to those in fully scripted situations.

Take one critical example. Rather than relying solely on clearly written job descriptions, senior executives engaged in improvisational planning must be willing to walk together into unfamiliar territory [referred to in an earlier article, "Leadership in Times of Uncertainty," as "map-making."]

This requires essential skills of improvisational, proactive planning such as higher levels of trust, open communication, mutual confidence, and an ability to read and react quickly to subtle cues. Like a championship basketball team, to know, through extensive practice, where each person is likely to be "coming from."

This latter point about "extensive practice" is particularly vital. To an audience—to organizations' customers and clients—a well-delivered improvisational performance is indistinguishable from a well-delivered, highly scripted one. In both cases, the audience presumes extensive rehearsals. In the case of implementing a well-formulated strategic plan, team development—if it occurs at all—will look more like football teams' practice sessions, which are focused on pre-determined content: the strategic plan.

In implementing an improvisational plan, players act more like a basketball team, which spends considerably more time working together on the process of how they handle emerging and evolving situations.

If your organization has to succeed on a highly unpredictable stage, developing these improvisational interpersonal and thinking skills are more than a luxury. They will determine whether you will successfully ride the next big wave or be swamped by it.

Week 12
A Human Plight

Illustrated by Dave Swann

Management theorists have been studying human motivation for decades. The hope was that managers could draw practical conclusions from this research to enable them to 'better motivate' employees as a stepping stone to improved productivity, morale and satisfaction.

As a result of these efforts, most of today's progressive managers are familiar with such fundamental theories as Abraham Maslow's "Hierarchy of Needs" and Frederick Hertzberg's "Two Factor Theory of Hygiene Versus Motivation", to name two of the more popular ones. While the existing theories vary in some ways, their underlying premise is the same: by treating people well, organizations would, in turn, do well.

However, when a recent study by The Herman Group of Greensboro, N.C., indicates that "30 percent to 40 percent of the working population is unhappy in their jobs to the extent they have 'checked our mentally and emotionally,'" we must step back and ask ourselves why. The simple explanation is that with everyone being asked to do more with less in the face of today's many workforce reductions, our theories of human motivation need to be revisited and revised. The problem, in my view, lies not with our theories. Human nature, fortunately, does not shift with the whims of the machinations of the Dow Jones.

No, the problem is more basic. It has to do with our deeply felt beliefs about why it is important to treat people well. It has to do, as the following story attest, with the reasons behind our efforts to treat people well in the first place. Our motives for efforts at motivating.

While at Massachusetts Institute of Technology I was fortunate to have had Douglas McGregor, the father of the "Theory X versus Theory Y" of human motivation, as a colleague. During a one of the skull sessions Doug held periodically with younger faculty members, he talked of a double bind he felt in his own professional career. In order to get the attention of the CEO's with whom he consulted, in order to motivate them to treat their people well, he would cite the many research studies he and others had conducted linking these efforts to reduced turnover, increased morale, and—under certain circumstances—increased productivity. In other words, he (and virtually everyone else like him) relied on hard logic and extrinsic linkages to make his point: treat your people well and your organization will do well.

"So what's the point?" you wonder. The problem, as he admitted with considerable embarrassment and hesitancy, was that—in his heart—he believed that the real reason to treat people well was intrinsic. In other words, the reason why you should empower your people by treating them with respect and trust (all the soft stuff our theories remind us about) is because they are human beings. And that is how human beings deserve to be treated. For their intrinsic, not extrinsic worth. Period.

As a result of doing so, and if you had faith—an unwavering belief that you were doing the right thing—more often than not, you (the organization) will be rewarded. When the going gets tough, people who are unconditionally cared for in this way will put out the extra effort to care in return. Why will they do their best? Because, as "Theory Y" so clearly laid out, it is in their human nature to do so.

However, as long as our primary motivation for seeking new ways to motivate employees is for extrinsic reasons—to gain control of them—the best we can hope for is that such efforts will 'capture' their minds and bodies. In order to deal with the '30 percent to 40 percent of our workforce that has checked our mentally and emotionally, we need to look for new ways to exhibit an intrinsic caring for one another.

We must capture an employee's heart and soul, the very creativity and innovation we need to survive and grow in today's competitive turbulent business environment.

Week 13
The "Carrot Versus The Stick"

Illustrated by Dave Swann

Motivating employees to do their best is always one of a manager's most significant challenges. This is particularly the case when your competitive advantage in a rapidly changing marketplace is based on a highly committed creative workforce.

It wouldn't take a rocket scientist (or even an expensive consultant!) to know immediately what's wrong with a picture from a Hagar the Horrible cartoon. One of Hagar's 'employees' is beating a mule's behind with a carrot while a stick hangs a few feet in front of the animal's nose. However, it is equally unclear that simply reversing the positions of carrot and the stick will really get the willingly offered heart-felt commitment needed to stay ahead of the competition versus the oft times begrudgingly offered minimal compliance that, at best, will keep your organization from falling far behind the competition.

Any manager at all familiar with modern theories of motivation knows this fact. Certain carrots—things like fair wages, meaningful benefits, and safe working conditions—will serve very well to satisfy needs that social scientists like Herzberg called hygiene factors. [Maslow referred to these as needs for food, safety, and security.] These same carrots, however, will do virtually nothing to activate the highest order needs for achievement and self-actualization upon which all striving for individual excellence—itself a necessary prerequisite of organizational excellence—is based.

So given the above, what can be done to tap into and direct our the needs for achievement and self-actualization that many social scientists believe lie dormant within everyone of us? The first factor of importance is to recognize that lower order needs are activated by extrinsic factors while higher order needs are activate by intrinsic factors. In other words, you do not 'motivate someone' to be self-actualizing. You do not literally grow a plant. Rather, you plant the seeds, nurture the soil, keep noxious weeds from choking it, and feed and water it.

You do the same thing with employees. You begin with the belief that they inherently need to achieve—to do the very best work of which they are capable—because they need to actualize their fullest selves. Then you do everything you can to act from that belief in how you deal with them. You actively involve them in setting challenging but achievable goals. You provide timely balanced feedback. You encourage risk taking and inculcate an attitude of learning from mistakes, not looking for scapegoats or people to blame. And, perhaps, the most difficult thing you can do is to sincerely invite and welcome any feedback they have for you as to how you can potentially change your own behavior to be the best 'gardener'—the best grower of talented employees you can be.

In other words, you make use of the known power of the self-fulfilling prophecy, wherein our beliefs are a major determinant of outcomes. Think about it. The effects of this phenomenon are unavoidable. So what can you really lose by treating your employees *as if* they did in fact—and they do—have a wide range of needs, from food to self-actualization.

When it comes to fully motivating your employees, it is not an *either or*, but rather a *yes and*. In other words, man may not work to his full potential for carrots alone, but neither will he work very well without them.

Week 14
The Bottom Line Of High Self-Esteem

Illustrated by David Swann

If I had a quarter for every time I've been asked: "What does all this 'touchy-feely stuff have to do with the bottom line?" the pile would look like I'd hit three cherries at Las Vegas. So let me see if I can boil the issue down to its simplest with reference to a two by two table

Self-esteem	High Certainty	High Uncertainty
High	Very High	High
Low	Moderately Low	Very Low

Our levels of self-esteem—our feelings about ourselves—directly influence a variety of factors; How confident we feel about our abilities to handle new and challenging tasks; the extent we are willing to take the moderate risks so characteristic of people with a desire to excel at whatever they do; the extent to which we can resist getting frozen by fear of the unknown; our willingness to think for ourselves, to offer ideas that might be opposite to those taken by the majority versus shrinking into the safety of the universal "We." In the jargon of the day, people with high self-esteem are often spoken of as "Having it all together."

So what does an individual's "having it all together" have to do with an organization's bottom line? The research is very clear. During periods of low organizational change, when things are relatively certain and predictable, people with high self-esteem clearly stand out above the rest. Their morale, productivity, and satisfaction—the steam engines of every organization's bottom line—are running at very high levels. In other words, they not only out-produce every one else, remain more loyal and take fewer sick days, they also do not poison the environment for others with the constant negativity and whining that characterizes their low morale colleagues.

However, as we are all too well aware, periods of low organizational change are few and far between these days. Turmoil, ambiguity, and uncertainty are more the soup de jour. Those with high self-esteem suffer the natural human consequences of these conditions—their productivity, morale, and satisfaction does drop a bit from very high to 'just' high. But their low self-esteem counterparts really fall apart with plummeting morale, satisfaction, and productivity figures.

To fully grasp the managerial implications of these repeated findings, we need to be certain we understand the fundamental roots of our feelings of self-esteem. They are, in a word, relationships. Let's take an extreme example. Have you ever seen a puppy dog sidle up to you when you reached out to pet it in a hesitant, fearful, butt-end first manner in anticipation of a rapid getaway? If you have, you've seen a puppy that has been very badly treated by someone.

To be sure, our feelings of self-worth can be traced to our childhoods. But current circumstances, specifically relationships with significant others—like managers—can and do activate old self-effacing scars where they exist. They also can and do activate new and more positive self-images. The Pygmalion Effect, the self-fulfilling prophecy, operates regardless of whether our beliefs and actions are self-esteem producing or self-defeat producing.

So if you're a CEO, sit back and ask yourself: Do you have any policies and procedures, which might be causing people to feel de-valued? Do you have any managers or supervisors who you know can be really verbally harsh sometimes? Does your organizational culture create win-win or win-lose dynamics among people?

For the facts are clear. Employees who are treated as valuable assets cannot help but be of greater value to you and to themselves. In other words, if your people are made to feel like winners, you can't lose.

Week 15
When Science Stops and 'Con-Science' Begins

"Conscience is first occupied with in ascertaining our duty, before we proceed to action; then in judging our actions when performed." [J.M. Mason]

I have enjoyed a four+ decade career teaching thousands of managers and leaders all I knew about the science and theory of win-win relationships. I have spent a six+ decade lifetime trying to successfully apply even a small number of those theories and scientific findings to my own day-to-day relationships. In this process, I have come to several conclusions about the key principles behind win-win relationships.

- They are simple to understand.

- They are difficult and not meant to be easy to apply.

- They can be applied more successfully with practice and feedback.

Let me expand for a moment on each of these points. The average person reading this book would have no trouble grasping the many theories of motivation, effective management, and leadership which abound in a massive and growing body of literature. Simply put they are not that complicated to understand…cognitively.

It comes as no surprise, however, I'm sure, that when it comes to applying the principles that are so easy to understand, I, like you, find them not so easy to actually use. I have, however, come to believe that they are not meant to be easy to apply. Why, you may wonder, are they "not meant to be easy to apply." The reason is that we are imperfect human beings. The difficulties we will encounter in learning to do what mountains of academic research and eons of personal experience tell us are the right things to do are the vehicles through which we are carried to a higher-order learning. We are given the opportunity to learn humility, acceptance, patience, tolerance, understanding, and the like. It is these most human of qualities that are the underpinning of the win-win relationships for which we struggle and hunger. The underpinnings of transformational and servant leadership.

Being human beings and not Gods, progress not perfection is our lot in lives. Feedback, as the third key principle above notes, is the key. Here again, we need only refer to a 'well-read' scientifically-based book [Rubin and Campbell, The ABCs of Effective Feedback: A Guide For Caring Professionals; Jossey-Bass, San Francisco, 1998, page 108-109] for eight 'commandments' of effective win-win feedback.

- Follow the KISS principle when you *describe*: keep it simple, stupid
- Be sure you *prescribe* does not ascribe.
- Avoid the rhetorical *ask* (a *prescribe* with a question mark).
- *Appreciate* your humanness; offer and accept apologies gracefully.
- When *attending* to someone, be fully present—this is the greatest gift we can offer.
- *Ask* abundantly—this is an act of affirmation and confirmation, not just a way of seeking information.
- Always check *understanding.*
- *Empathize* before you criticize or moralize.

The best that science has to offer will most certainly contribute to a better understanding of the 'whats' and 'hows' of effective management and leadership. Do everything you can to embrace as much of that material as you can. However, the day and the moment will come when all of the science, the theory, and even all of the hard practice you've done and feedback you've sought seem woefully inadequate. Because what you are facing is not a book. Not an experimental subject buried in a University laboratory. Not a static statistically significant 2x2 table. You are facing another unpredictable, imperfect, fallible human being.

So, based on my own experience, under those circumstances you might consider the following. Pause for a split second. Try to put "all that science out of your mind." Get quiet. Look deeply into your heart—your conscience—and ask yourself; "What is the very best thing I can do or say in this situation?" Neale Donald Walsch's way of saying this same thing was so simple and so powerful: "What would God do or say now?" If you don't get a strong feeling of 'right and wrong' wherever it is in your person that you 'know' your conscience resides, I have one final suggestion.

Consider the possibility that the best thing to do at the moment is to do nothing.

Week 16
Losing Focus

Illustrated by Bryant Fukutomi

The February 2002 issue of the *Harvard Business Review* reported a startling research finding that warns of danger: "Fully 90 percent of managers squander their time in all sorts of ineffective activities. In other words, a mere 10 percent of managers spend their time in a committed, purposeful, and reflective manner."

Since managers are responsible for ensuring that the organization is getting a maximal return on investment on its most important asset—its human resources—these findings are particularly worrisome. They suggest that instead of leveraging their actions by spending their own time in ways that make the largest difference for the most people, managers may have lost their focus. While each manager will need to do his or her own cost/benefit assessment, here are a few managerial traps to consider that I've seen in my own experience.

The first has to do with the difference between "doing" and "managing." Many technical people, for example, have been promoted to managerial positions because they were very good at solving complex impersonal (i.e., non-human) problems. Add to this ability their genuine love for solving such problems, and the newly lean structures of most organizations these days, and you have the ingredients for why many managers spend long hours behind closed doors putting out the fires that others should be handling. Yes, these managers are committed and hard working, but are they effectively making the bigger differences expected of them?

The bigger differences I'm talking about have to do with managerial accountabilities like coaching and succession planning. Successful coaches spend lots of time observing, making themselves visible, and developing the kinds of open relationships that allow people to seek help from them and receive feedback. Management by walking around is not being nosy. It has nothing to do with being untrusting of your people, but everything to do with successful coaching. And successful coaching is itself a prerequisite to growing successors for your own position.

Having said that, there is one vitally important reason not to be walking around all the time. In the research results quoted above, it is noted that very few managers spend any time in a reflective manner. In other words, because we often don't distinguish activity from impact, or busy-ness from productivity, we also seriously endanger one of our most valuable human resources which is the ability to learn from our experiences.

When was the last time you scheduled a few hours time to sit back and do some quiet reflection on where you and your team have been lately? Or when did you and your entire team last take such time together? Not very recently, if at all. And, even though you know that reflection is the key to learning, if you did take the time, it's highly likely you still felt twinges of guilt, as if you weren't "really working," weren't really earning your pay.

Furthermore, when it does take place, such learning time is focused solely on diagnosing the underlying causes of mistakes. And rightfully so, as repeating mistakes is most assuredly an example of squandering time. But it's equally important to be able to learn from your successes. In all my years of teaching in management graduate schools, I saw hundreds of courses on the management skill of problem solving, but not one that focused on the management of success. It's my contention that a greatly overlooked source of squandered time is this lost opportunity to diagnose the exact causes of successes and therefore the knowledge of how to best replicate and expand on them.

Maybe it's about time to do a managerial time-utilization inventory. If 90 percent of [your] managers are squandering their time in all sorts of ineffective activities, you can be certain that the people who are reporting to them are doing no better.

Week 17
Learning to Learn

Illustrated by Dave Swann

Many of us are familiar with the following piece of sage advice: "Give a man a fish and you feed him for a day. Teach him how to fish and you feed him for a lifetime." A recent conversation with a CEO colleague of mine brought to light an entirely new slant on this age-old wisdom.

She was frustrated because she knew she was not relating as well to her vice presidents as they or she would have liked. Every time she tried to do what she thought would make the situation better, it would work for a while only to revert shortly thereafter. She threw up her hands and lamented: "I want to learn, but it just seems like I can't. You're my coach! What should I do?"

To her credit, my response—"Perhaps we need to work more on your teach-ability before you'll experience the rewards you seek from your efforts to learn."—did not lead her to show me the door.

Making ourselves open to being taught is akin to doing the work farmers must do to prepare their fields before planting new crops. There are several attitudes and beliefs that, if they are not "weeded out," can easily act to choke off the sustainability of any well-motivated attempts to learn something new.

Perfectionism is one attitude that seriously erodes teachability. Progress and steady improvement are the best we can ever hope for. If we continue to expect or believe in perfection, the first sign of normal ups and downs can sap our energy and motivation. Mistakes become self-defeating vs. self-motivating.

Further, I tried to help her see that sometimes an old habit must be uprooted or pruned in order to make room for a new one. If your success to date has been built on your ability to come up with your own solutions to problems—the faster, the better—helping your people learn how to figure out their own solutions is going to be a challenge for you. Like a tennis player with an overdeveloped forehand stroke, you will need to make some conscious efforts to bring your backhand into play.

Because those muscles are a bit rusty, they bring us back face-to-face with our first point above: the need to tolerate slow progress and not expect immediate perfection. The reward, of course, for going through this period where our teachability is being stressed is that we add a new skill to our own behavioral repertoire.

The third set of issues that affect our readiness, willingness and ability to be taught are more psychological but nonetheless vital.

In her frustration at having done everything she could think of on her own to solve her problem, my colleague finally surrendered to a fundamental fact of our human natures when she lamented, "What should I do?"

While it might sound like an improbable conundrum, relationship-oriented problems, by their nature, cannot be resolved alone. They require the reliance on a relationship. In other words, left to her own devices, my colleague could only expect to get similar results.

So, in asking for help, my colleague had to make herself vulnerable. She had to admit she was imperfect; else she'd have been able to solve the problem by herself. And a healthy dash of humility had to be added alongside a well-deserved reservoir of pride and self-confidence.

So we can now return to our opening piece of wisdom and reframe it in terms that speak directly to the challenge of management development: Give me a skill and I'm more effective today. Help me learn how to be more teachable, and I can be more effective for a lifetime."

Week 18
Management with a Mission

Illustrated by Dave Swann

Individuals who are severely depressed dread opening their normally sleep-deprived eyes in the morning. Rather than the dawning of a new day full of untold exciting possibilities and opportunities, their days all look dark. They have come to expect an ever-deepening spiral of despair, fueled by the sense of having no real sense of purpose in their lives. If it gets really too much to handle, one day they just stop investing in life, or worse, they 'quit!'

'Sad, to be sure.' you think, but what has anomie got to do with managerial and organizational excellence? The answer is quite simple. Just watch the eyes of many a senior management team roll over when it is suggested that they need to work on the two dreaded M and V words: mission and values. They would rather try to sail around on the turbulent seas of ambiguity and uncertainty—which characterize today's business environment—like a ship without a rudder, buffeted by competitive waves they didn't see coming. They would rather adopt reactive verses proactive stances toward important changes. Little wonder so many of today's employees have stopped investing their hearts and souls into their jobs.

They bring their bodies to work to serve their time, but emotionally they have quit their jobs.

When one of my clients asked me: "How can a really clear unambiguous mission and value statement counteract this kind of organizational anomie?" I told the following story.

As many business travelers do, I have a bad habit of trying to over-stuff my carry on bag. So when the zipper on my Lands End bag gave out, I was upset, but not surprised.

After explaining my problem to the customer service person on the phone, and even admitting [albeit a bit sheepishly] that I had caused it myself by [over-stuffing the bag], I simply asked how I could get it repaired. I was quickly told that all I needed to do was return the old bag and a new one would be sent to me immediately, free of charge! And as if that wasn't enough to really get my attention, I could have my initials embroidered on my new bag; again, free of charge. Why? Because I'd been so thoughtful as to take my time to bring the problem [the one, recall, that I caused!] to their attention.

My own bit of follow-up research, in the form of a letter to the President of Lands End, yielded the following. The senior management of Lands End had spent considerable time and energy to create a mission that would a) engage the hearts and minds of all employees, and b) empower all employees to know what the right decision was when they had to act on their own.

Their results after long, apparently pointless dialogue? "Guaranteed. Period." My bag was guaranteed, for life, even against damage I inflicted. Period. By my taking the time to let them know what had happened, I was actually helping them to fulfill their mission and values. And what is particularly amazing about that story is that it took place 15 years ago! And I still remember it! And I still spread the good word by telling others about it. That's the real power of such mission and value statements. They stick in everyone's minds, employees and customers alike.

And, if you need any more proof as to the power of the dreaded M and V words, try this simple test. See how long it takes you to match up the following five missions and value statements with their respected enterprises: Walt Disney; Wal-Mart; Merck; Mary Kay Cosmetics, and 3M.

"To solve unsolved problems innovatively."
"To give unlimited opportunities to women."
"To preserve and improve life."

"To give ordinary folk the chance to buy the same thing as rich people."

"To make people happy."

Week 19
Save Us From Help

Illustrated by David Swann

There is hardly a service industry today that is not trying to get its customers to do more and more via the Web. From airlines competing with travel agents to banks trying to reduce the number of human resources, the promises are similar. The cost savings from fast and efficient service will be passed along to the consumer in the way of lower prices.

Alongside that rhetoric, here's an example of the reality that goes along with a local organization's efforts to motivate just such behavior in the form of doing all your banking electronically.

A client of mine in Europe recently asked me if I'd prefer to have them send a check to cover my work or just deposit it electronically. Doing it electronically would cost them some moneys, but they were more than willing to do so because they so valued our relationship. A "no brainer" for me. Or so it seemed until my Office Manager noticed that our local bank where we've been doing business for over 25 years (the same one that is spending huge amounts of advertising money to motivate us to bank electronically) charged $25.00 to receive and process the electronic transfer.

During my next visit to the bank I explained my disappointment at what had happened. Response? A 'robotic'; "That's our policy, sir." Then I asked what it would have cost me if I had deposited a check for that amount personally. Response? "It wouldn't have cost anything, sir." Followed by another wonderfully programmed robotic response [I was obviously not the first to ask these questions!]: "But you would not have been able to draw on those funds for several working days."

Imagine that! For the mere sum of $25.00, I was able to draw upon funds sitting in the Bank of England immediately versus having to wait for several days.

This experience led me to dig through my files for an old Web story, a small portion of which follows

>>><<<

What if bank customers issued the following statements? Henceforth, the authorized contact person at the bank is the only one with whom I shall deal. [Please note that a Notary Public must countersign copies of all of his/her medical history and financial details.] In due course, I will issue this person a PIN number, which will be 28 digits in length. This person may call me at anytime and their call will be answered by my automated voice service.

On the matter of costs ongoing drive for greater efficiency comes at a cost, which you have always been quick to pass onto me. Let me repay your kindness by passing some costs back. Inquiries from the authorized contact will be billed at $5 per minute of my time spent in response. My new automated phone service runs at 75 cents per minute so you'd be advised to keep your inquiries brief and to the point. Regrettably, but again following your example, I must levy and establishment fee to cover setting up this new arrangement.

>>><<<

There is an important challenge, underlying this all to familiar scenario.

Customer service people, it would appear, seldom use themselves as the guinea pigs for the systems they design. And even if they do test their own system, it is only a test to see if it works. That is not the same as having to use it day after day. Senior executives have VIP numbers that get them around their own systems. No pressing buttons and listening to Muzak for them. And I doubt if too many airline executives use their Websites to get reservations or sit in one of the sardine cans called a seat when they do fly.

Customer service systems are becoming increasingly de-humanizing systems. The only way to humanize them is for the senior executives in the organizations that have them, and the people who design them, to have to use them day-in and day-out. Like the rest of us.

Empathy is the best form of service. As long as it doesn't come pre-recorded from a new button I can press.

Week 20
Corporate Culture Should Not Be Neglected When Nurturing Startups

Illustrated by Jaime Ubongen

Research tells us that fully 70 percent of the fundamental values and beliefs that guide our behaviors later in our lives are inculcated into our personalities before we reach first or second grade. This does not mean that who we are is irrevocably set in stone as a result of our early childhood experiences. An open inquiring mind enables beliefs and prejudices to change with changing circumstances. We always have choices about how to behave. But it does mean that learning a new habit, particularly one that will be replacing an existing one, is very difficult because it requires the unlearning of an existing ingrained habit first. Changing old habits creates more resistance to change than learning a new habit tabla rosa.

The same principle is true when it comes to organizational cultures. Many large corporations find themselves needing to dramatically change their organizational personalities if they are to survive and grow in an increasingly uncertain market place.

They are not in the position of starting fresh to create a new culture. In many cases, they have decades of proud tradition. In striving to define and successfully inculcate new cultural dimensions into the organization's blood stream—itself and incredibly challenging task, as many can attest—they have the added challenge of not throwing out the baby with the bath water.

In discussing this issue recently over lunch with a colleague, we realized a potentially untapped unique contribution the small business community could make. New entrepreneurial start-ups—of exactly the kind many cities are striving to attract and develop—need to be viewed in a manner analogous to youngsters in the formative years. The roots of their organizational personalities are being set in motion in their early stages of growth and development. These corporate cultures are clearly known and documented to be a major factor in determining long-range sustainability and success in the marketplace.

The problem, however, is that this natural process of culture development is going unmanaged for several reasons.

One, the excitement of being involved in something new and promising encourages the founding personnel and their generally small cadre of employees to sweep a lot of normal growing pains under the carpet. In so doing, the organization is inadvertently creating a weakened foundation from which its culture will emerge—not unlike what would happen if we built a home on a termite infested set of cross-beams.

Two, very few small start-ups have the discretionary capital needed to fund organizational development. All of their time, energy and resources seem to have to be earmarked for survival. When asked about the need for activities like team building, conflict resolution training and the like, many will agree whole-heartedly as to their importance.

And in the next breath they will make a verbal commitment to put them higher on the priority list…as soon as circumstances permit. Two dangers exist in this very normal pattern: (1) many a small entrepreneurial venture fails because of the termites it has ignored in its human foundation. And (2) should the organization succeed, it will then have to face the even more expensive and time-consuming challenge of remaking an existing culture.

If the powers to be in any state—e.g. the Chamber of Commerce and state government—are really serious about nurturing the creation and sustainability of new ventures, some thought should be given to how best to support the development of strong and healthy organizational cultures in their formative years.

Such efforts would not only help to create stronger small businesses, but could also be expected to shed some new insights on how larger corporations might go about the process of culture change, one small unit at a time.

Week 21
Don't Be A Dumbo

Illustrated by David Swann

It seems that when training a young elephant to work, the first thing the trainer does is place a heavy manacle and chain around its leg, and then secures the chain to a stake driven deep into the ground. Moving freely and escape are severely curtailed.

It doesn't take the baby elephant very long to get the message. Its working life becomes more comfortable, less painful, as long as it a) stops wasting energy trying to operate outside its "managerially prescribed," limited range of influence, and b) passively allows its "manager" to make all decisions. What is even more amazing to that, once these beliefs are internalized, the elephant can be transported to and employed at an entirely new "job site," with only a very thin rope to remind it "who is the boss around here."

The parallel managerial challenges are clear. Let's look at a few.

You've hired a new young employee, a real "go-getter" ready to set the world on fire and show everyone what he has learned in his recently completed MBA program.

Having been there yourself, you know the dangers of just letting him run loose. In his youthful inexperience, he can inadvertently end up leaving others feeling "stampeded" and resentful at this "Young Turk" who has all the answers.

You know that what you ought to do is take some real quality time to walk him around, show him the ropes, and be available to answer a ton of questions, to be his hands-on coach.

But because you are up to your eyeballs in your own mountains of work and e-mails, if you're not careful, what can end up happening is one of two things:

(1) You may send the person out to the trenches, a 6-inch thick orientation manual in hand, to sink or swim. If so, be prepared to have to deal with the consequences of the normal mistakes he is likely to make. Ask yourself honestly: How do you react to these expected early mistakes? Do you, in effect, "crack a whip?" Do you summarily "yank them back?"

(2) You may, to protect the person and yourself, send him out to the trenches on a really tight leash. You start with micro-managing him and warning him to "Go slowly. Be careful." Check with me before you do anything "significant'." (Whatever that means!)

If you adopt either of these kinds of strategies, the die may be cast. An enormous reservoir of strength and desire to contribute, like a baby elephant, may be being conditioned to "play it safe."

While we may not initially see it, this same dynamic can be set in motion with other newcomers. In this case, instead of a "Young Turk," you've hired a seasoned veteran. You know the kind—someone like one of those, "special players" a professional sports team hires late in their career. The missing piece who will get the championship they've been missing. Big signing bonus. No trade clauses in a sweet contract. Decades of deferred compensation.

In the business world, analogous contracts used to bring very senior people to large corporations can take on the qualities of the manacle and chain around the elephant's foot. We know that more than 50 percent of a broad spectrum of America's middle management and general work force is just "hanging around and marking time" until they can retire. One can only wonder how many more senior executives are just marking time. Playing it safe. Staying low on the radar screen until their stock options come to fruition. Indeed, "golden parachutes" can become "golden handcuffs."

It may behoove you to take a good hard look at both your own managerial behavior and some of your organization's personnel policies and procedures and ask yourself: Are we inadvertently training our "most valuable assets" to act like trusted creative thinkers or like elephants?

Week 22
Helping Others Grow

Illustrated by David Swann

"Originally the word *power*," a noted Buddhist philosopher tells us in "The Book of Awakening by Mark Nepo" meant "to be able to be." In time, it was contracted to mean "to be able." We suffer the difference."

Recent and continuing political crises, as well as the misuse and abuse of corporate funds by those in positions of significant power, also serve as painful reminders of the all too many instances where the word power means "to be mean."

But there is a new generation of senior corporate leaders who are embracing and acting from the positive face of power. Leaders like Tim Sanders of Yahoo who speak of "love as being the most powerful force in business." Leaders like Mark Cuban, the young Internet billionaire, whose motto with respect to the treatment of customers was "Make love, not war."

This trend, while it may seem radical to some, is actually predictable given the results of a study conducted by the highly respected Center for Creative Leadership. No. 1 on the list of the top four leadership demands in the coming decades was employee development. Note that this is not a demand that will be delegated to the human resources department. It is a demand that will become a leader's direct responsibility, and presumably area of accountability.

In other words, the leaders of the future are going to have to learn how, as a part of their operational line responsibilities, to help others grow to become the best people they can be. Which, as you may recall, is what Sanders reminded us is tantamount to learning how to "be loving."

If such direct terminology gives you chicken skin, try an analogy. Think of the challenge as being akin to being a good farmer. You have to till the soil. Start with a strong seedling (which you can expect your HR department to help you locate). Keep the weeds of bureaucratic red tape from choking it to death. Be sure to give it sunshine, water, and, if need be, even some fertilizer. (By which we mean, just to be clear, periodic special projects that feed its need for booster shots).

And when it needs more room to grow than you maybe able to provide in your field, don't try to hang on just because it serves your needs. Rather, help transplant it to someone else's patch where it has the chance to grow even bigger and stronger.

And do so not because you expect a quid pro quo in return.

Why?

Because doing something out of love means you do it because it is the right thing to do. And, as many can attest, the less you expect in return for acts of love, acts of generosity—be they professional or personal—the more you will receive, in kind, in return.

Simply put, learn to care for and about your people like you know you would have to learn to care about and for your crops if you wanted to be a successful farmer.

Recognize and accept that learning to care for and about another person is synonymous with developing highly refined sophisticated interpersonal skills. You can't have one without the other.

Furthermore, it is the very absence of these interpersonal skills that is the No. 1 cause of what the Center For Creative Leadership identified as the key derailment factor causing high-potential leaders to falloff the fast track, fast!

So the reasons for not using your power as a leader as a means to control people and situations are clear. As are the positive reasons for developing your 'soft skills' so you can use your power to help propel people to even greater heights of achievement.

The next time you face your senior team, and or one of your colleagues, make a conscious choice about which of your two faces of power you want to put forward.

Week 23
Authority, Accountability And Responsibility Can Be A Finely Balanced Trio

Illustrated by Jaime Ubongen

In order to keep pace with the uncertainty and rapid change that have become "business as usual" in today's competitive global market place, organizations are being forced to re-examine some fundamental managerial principles. In working with a multinational client recently on the challenge of managing globally based virtual teams, we found ourselves taking a hard look at the relationship between authority, accountability, and responsibility.

My mulling led me, as it usual does, first to my dictionary. Authority, I discovered, is "the influence of character or office." The authority of "office", I was reminded, is rooted in the "power to enforce obedience or command action." "Character," on the other hand, derives its power from "opinion, respect or esteem." Putting those pieces together adds clarity to part of our formula; we have choices as to the sources from which we can draw our authority.

It came as no surprise to see that to be accountable is to be "answerable to a superior." What did surprise me—pleasantly, I must say—was the example usage which followed immediately: "as in every person is accountable to God [their own conscience] for their conduct." (The bracketed is my own addition.)

The definition of responsible, to finish our trip through Webster's, was: "answerable or accountable as being the cause, agent or source of something." And that *something*, I learned a few lines later, is the "ability to distinguish right from wrong, and therefore be accountable for one's own behavior."

So, all you 'traditionalists' can breath a sigh of relief. The good news is that the formula does hold. Authority, responsibility, and accountability can form, if they are carefully aligned, three sides of an equilateral triangle. The challenge, of course, lies in the word "aligned," for it reminds us of the fundamental choices only we can make as to what "figures" we plug into this formula.

For example, if the only source of authority with which I can comfortably function is that of "office and the power to enforce obedience or command action," then my posture toward accountability and responsibility has certain predictable elements. The organization's formal hierarchy would be of great importance to me…in both directions. As a manager, I would frequently reflect the "golden rule": "Those who control the gold make the rules." My direct reports, as a consequence, could be expected to lament at how little time and energy I spend explaining the whys and wherefores of my decisions (since I control the gold!)

On the other hand, if I can learn to be comfortable using the authority of my "character and the power of opinion, respect or esteem" of myself and of others, then the formal hierarchy—while I respect the fact that it has to exist and has a role to play—is not primary. Rather, the "superior" to whom I am primarily accountable is a power higher than my need to "play god," a desire driven by ego. The ultimate responsibility for my ability to "distinguish right from wrong" is, and will remain, in my heart, in my conscience.

I believe these choices, shed considerable light on the managerial tensions many are experiencing. For the overwhelming majority of us, our life experiences have been in organizational cultures—including families—where "enforcement by obedience to superiors" was the dominant modality. As painful as it may be, it is nonetheless comfortable and familiar.

Yet, growing needs for globally dispersed virtual teams, rapid responses to environmental changes, and the flexibility to remain fluid and adaptive, are driving organizations to rely less and less on the comfort and familiarity of hierarchy, office and command.

Rather, regardless of a person's position in the hierarchy, people are being challenged to become empowered.

And what can empowerment mean other than using the personal "power of opinion, respect or esteem" to become the "cause, agent or source of *something*". That something being the doing of what in their hearts they know is "right from wrong."

The new formula equating authority, responsibility and accountability has little to do with position, obedience, and ego.

It is all about personal integrity, humility and win-win relationships where one becomes skilled in being accountable for one's own behavior.

Week 24
No Excuse For Work Abuse

Illustrated by Bryant Fukutomi

There's a bumper sticker that never fails to send a shiver down my spine. It reminds us that there is absolutely no excuse for domestic violence. None. The last time I saw it, I found myself wondering what difference it could make if we started to think about and act toward our work places as if they were our families.

They are, after all, the social systems in which we spend more than one-third of our waking hours as adults! Here are a few examples of what came to mind.

Let's tackle to issue of violence first. Imagine a loved one of yours is being treated for a somewhat serious health condition in Average Hospital XYZ. The nurse caring for your loved one is one of the 2500 nurses nation wide recently surveyed about the extent to which they experience and or observe firsthand a variety of forms of abusive behavior. These acts of violence ranged from condescending and disparaging remarks to fits of anger resulting in the throwing of medical charts and or equipment.

This caregiver may be one of the almost 35 percent who reported weekly or daily occurrences of such abuse. The primary perpetrators of this abuse were less than 10 percent of their colleagues, all of whose identities were well known. In describing how they coped with such a constant barrage of abuse, most simply shrugged their shoulders and said: "You learn to have thick skin and get used to it." Do you want a thick-skinned nurse taking care of your loved one?

Suppose now this same loved one with being rushed into the ER of the same Average Hospital XYZ, but now with a life-threatening illness. Matters of seconds can be the difference between living, becoming a vegetable, or dying. Would you be 'interested' in knowing whether the attending physician and nurse were carrying the weight of an unresolved interpersonal conflict on their minds and in their hearts? You bet you would. Hard evidence confirms that such tensions—exactly the kind that go along with frequent, and excused or tolerated, verbal abuse—are highly correlated with whether ER patients with life-threatening illnesses live or die.

Healthcare too close to home? Take a moment to think about the number of businesses that have been ruined because the 'parents' heading up those organizations' manipulated information about profits. Values of full and open disclosure, the way good parents try to teach their children to communicate, were replaced by two sets of books. Face-to-face honesty and ethical integrity were replaced by bald-faced lying and manipulative press releases. Equitably sharing whatever profits were available was replaced by "we'll take ours and leave you with crumbs."

Aside from the direct consequences of these types of examples what is most insidious is the flood of excuses, made to justify and rationalize the actions; with virtually no personal accountability. There are a mere nine words that make up almost 25 percent of everything we say. They are: and, be, have, it, of, the, to, will, you. One word is conspicuously absent. The word is **I**!

So the next time you see something wrong taking place, at home or in your work place, ask yourself: What difference can **I** make?

Edward Everett Hale gave us the answer: "I am only one, but still I am one. I cannot do everything, but still I can do something. And because I cannot do everything, I will not refuse to do something that I can do."

Week 25
Cooperation: A Form Of Mutual Altruism

Illustrated by Dave Swann

I'm not certain we needed a major research study from the University of California-Los Angeles to prove the following point. Finding your paper in your garage on a Sunday morning, almost automatically adding 15% to your bill in a restaurant, producing a new commercial jet liner, and managing a state government of have one thing in common: They are dependent upon cooperation among relative strangers.

What was particularly disturbing, to this observer, was the fact that the concept used in the study to explain this glue that holds all social systems together was "altruistic punishment."

Talk about an oxymoron. A quick trip through Webster's yields the following. "The principle or practice of unselfish concern for the welfare of others (as opposed to egoism)" has been joined with "to handle or treat roughly, harshly; to hurt." To be sure, the second definition of altruism listed is: "behavior by an animal that may be to its disadvantage but that benefits others of its kind."

The essence of their argument is that 'altruistic punishers' are willing to stick their heads into the lion's den. Specifically, they are willing to confront members of a group to stop behavior that might hurt the group, even if by doing so the confrontation costs them something personally.

When it comes to applying this concept to organizations, whose achievement of excellence is greatly influenced by people's voluntary willingness, and ability, to cooperate, there are several things wrong with this way of thinking. Confrontation, for example, is portrayed as something bad, which it is not. Confrontation simple means putting one's heads together in the service of achieving a common goal. It is the ability to manage confrontation and conflict, which is essential to realizing its positive potential. When employees have been given the skills they need, they can have healthy productive confrontations. They can form and maintain win-win relationships, and punishment altruistic or otherwise, has absolutely no place in such relationships.

Furthermore, we are neither laboratory animals nor the mathematical simulations used to test this theory. We are human beings. We are empowered with the ability to make conscious choices. In any given moment, we can elect to be egotistical; to manifest unselfish concern for our fellow human beings; to be rough, harsh, and hurtful; and, even, as past and recent history have reminded us, to be unbelievably torturous and cruel. Along with this freedom to choose comes the accountability for the consequences.

Managers can choose to berate challenging employees or to confront them as fellow human beings struggling to do their best. In both cases they should expect reactions and responses that are related to their own behaviors as managers. We are all 100 percent accountable for our 50 percent of every relationship. Or more simply, what goes around, comes around, be it punishment or altruism.

Finally, let's return to altruism. We need look no further than the 250,000 Americans who risked their lives to free the people of Iraq to be reminded that we are capable of incredibly unselfish acts of altruism. When Saint Francis of Assisi said: "It is better to strive to comfort than be comforted, to understand than to be understood, to love than to be loved," he was offering us an ideal toward which we can strive. But we are human beings, not saints. We need to both understand and be understood, to comfort and be comforted, to love and be loved. In other words, being human means we need to be able to have it both ways.

So once again we are brought to an earlier point. Cooperation may be hard-wired into our emotional systems, and it is certainly essential to the success of any organization. But we don't need punishment, of others or of ourselves, to ensure altruistic confrontation. What we need are constant opportunities to fine-tune and hone our skills at manifesting our cooperative human natures.

Week 26
Trust—Once You Lose It, It's Hard To Regain

Illustrated by David Swann

When my wife and I bought our home, the bank required a full termite inspection before a mortgage would be granted. When the report came back: "No active termites," the bank issued us the loan we need to complete the purchase. It wasn't until we moved into our home and began some renovations that we realized that the operative word in the bank's abstract report was <u>active</u>.

The reason why there were "No active termites," was because virtually all the internal studs that were hidden from easy visual observation had already been eaten away. The termites had left for greener pastures.

In retrospect, we should have been a bit wary, as the mortgage was given on the value of our land, and the house was noted to be of virtually no value! But the bank was totally within their rights. They were under no legal obligation to tell me any more than they did.

As I have listened to executive after executive talk about how important trust among and between all staff is to their own organization's ability to achieve excellence, I have often found myself reflecting on my house experience. So in the next series of chapters, we will address the issue of trust, its easily visible—and not-so-easily visible—impact on the all important quality of the relationships that determine any organization's ability to achieve excellence.

The first thing we must acknowledge is that trust, without clear behavioral specification, is one of those abstract ideals that can be debated, ad infinitum, to little avail.

My bank did nothing 'untrustworthy,' in the legal sense of the term. So why did I mistrust them immediately after gaining full knowledge of the truth? Because I felt they 'knowingly' withheld information from me for self-serving reasons. I felt they violated a moral trust, a fiduciary trust. In other words, they assumed—I assumed—that I might not purchase the house and, therefore, not borrow their money—money, which, at the time in 1981 carried an 18-plus percent interest rate!

Several things of importance about this complicated multi-faceted concept of trust are reflected in this last paragraph. While trust and honesty are bedmates, I cannot accuse my loan officer of being dishonest, untrustworthy. She did not lie to me. She merely was implementing organizational policy.

To be sure, I could have asked. But when you are unknowing, when you don't even know enough to know what to ask, it is a time of increased need to trust in the first place.

So point number one about trust is that what we call interpersonal trust, albeit it related to, is separate and distinct from organizational trust.

As an employee, you may feel your own supervisor is perfectly trustworthy, however you define that in specific behavioral terms, and still feel that your "organization" is not.

Policies and procedures that facilitate unfair unequal treatment of employees (hiring, performance appraisal, promotion, etc.) will, like termites, erode a sense of organizational trust. And, as Robert Galford and Anne Drapeau ("Enemies of Trust," Harvard Business Review, February 2003) note: "If people think an organization acted in bad faith, they'll rarely forgive, and they never forget."

However, while this distinction between system levels and interpersonal levels of trust is useful, it begs an essential point. There is no such thing as an "organizational policy or procedure" separate from the individuals who created them in the first place and decided to maintain them thereafter.

When certain individuals—those in positions of higher power—allow themselves to create policies and procedures that erode an employee's sense of organizational trust, they are contributing to what we all recognize as familiar "we-they" dynamics.

Those who feel "violated," "threatened" and "mistrustful" in some way by what "they" have done to "us" bond together.

All of "us" and all of "them" trust one of our own more than we trust one of them, sometimes blindly.

We need only recall any recent labor strike we've endured to be reminded that the result of these ever-widening trust gaps are a lose-lose.

Week 27
Trust—Needs A Strong Foundation

Illustrated by Bryant Fukutomi

A colleague of mine, Jack Silversin, has reframed the notion of enemies of trust as "trust busters." I find that notion more meaningful, since it captures a painful truth. Building trust can be an agonizingly slow process, while destroying it can appear to occur in a split second.

Why "appear?" Because the sense of trust may have been teetering, may have been eroding from the foundation up, for a while, even before the "straw that broke the camel's back" became manifest.

Let's look at a few examples. A corporate town meeting to discuss the details of a rumored merger was scheduled three weeks ago. But each time, the day beforehand, it was rescheduled to the following week. Always justified with the reason: "We have some further analyses to do." Meanwhile, the rumors about how big the layoffs would be if there was a merger grew exponentially.

So when the chief executive finally stood up at the town meeting, confirmed the merger and announced: "Every effort will be made to ensure a place is found for everyone," eyes darted back-and-forth and rolled back as if to say, "Yeah, and if you believe that, we have a bridge in Brooklyn we'd like to sell you!"

Inconsistent, abstract messages that feed rumors will, like termites, eventually erode trust. It is hard to imagine that employees will give this CEO the benefit of the many doubts they will have over the coming months.

A second example has to do with obvious double standards. It is not unusual in a health care organization to have one or two physicians who regularly verbally abuse the staff with whom they work. Because these physicians are typically also among the organization's biggest producers—often adding several millions of dollars gross business—the medical director, chief of staff, and other key administrators often adopt a posture of, "See no evil, hear no evil."

The corrosive effects of this trust-busting dynamic of double standards spreads far and wide. Motivation among deserving employees must suffer. Why? Because there is simply no honest answer to the question they will ask themselves, or ask aloud: "Why should I break my back if so-and-so can continue to get away with their behavior and still get all the same benefits?"

Supervisors who try to discipline their own employees will increasingly find themselves having martyr-like, whining conversations like those we all can recall having had with our teenage children: "Why do I have to do that if he doesn't?"

I was reminded of a third example recently as I was facilitating an off-site senior executive planning retreat. One of the group's members was missing, having announced her "early retirement" the day before the meeting. She had been having a very rocky time getting along with the CEO for months, so her leaving was not unexpected.

I watched carefully for the first 30 minutes or so as the group settled down and began to work through their agenda. They were flat and cautious, a bad combination any time, particularly for a vital strategic planning retreat.

There was clearly a red elephant on the table that no one was willing to discuss. When I offered that thought, the first reaction I got was feigned confusion.

A more direct approach was needed. So I asked everyone to take a few moments to jot down the facts, assumptions and fears they had about so-and-so 's departure.

The discussion that followed uncovered several previous red elephants that had eroded the team's sense of trust in one another, and themselves. Had we just driven our way through this history, their new strategic plan might have been, as Harry Bellefonte warns us, "A house build on a weak foundation."

The catch 22, of course, is that it takes courage and trust to identify and work on dynamics like inconsistent messages, double standards and red elephants that are eroding trust.

Week 28
Rebuilding Trust

Illustrated by Star-Bulletin

In the previous couple of articles, we have noted two things about trust: 1) Without behavioral specification, it is an abstract ideal; and 2) It is slow to grow and rapid to deteriorate.

While we may wish that our trust was never betrayed, our fallible human natures guarantee that times will come when we need to deal with re-building trust (both as the betrayer and the betrayee!) Suddenly, like needing to decide whether to hire an admitted felon who has paid his debt for a past crime, trust becomes much more concrete than abstract.

Several decades ago, one of my sons, who had just received his driver license, failed to fulfill an agreement we had about his use of the family car. He arrived home, considerably later than agreed upon, without any call at all. He violated my trust.

I recall making the mistake of asking, "Why were you late?" The result was a string of rational-sounding explanations I had trouble believing for a very simple reason. It is hard to trust the explanations of someone who has acted in an untrustworthy manner. Shifting to asking, "How did it happen?" helped a bit to reduce his defensiveness and my chagrin. The critical shift came when I moved to: "Well, here's what I expect in the future."

I then proceeded to lay out a very clear set of conditions, which included a reiteration of a clear agreement before leaving the house as to when he'd be home. However, a codicil was added with the requirement that he call home when he was leaving wherever he was, to assure me he'd be able to be home at the agreed upon time.

When he balked, "But that means you don't trust me!" I took a deep breath before responding.

I affirmed that I wanted to trust him again, and that there was a consequence to his having abused that trust. Specifically, we'd both have to accept that, for a period of time, he'd have to work to regain my trust. Once we agreed on how long the new condition would be in effect, we were able to move forward.

Let me use a medical analogy to explain what I believed we did.

Imagine that a violated trust is like an emotional broken leg. Left to its own devices, a broken leg will heal itself. (Ergo, the old adage that time heals all wounds.) The problem, however, is that it is most likely to heal in a crooked fashion. The body upon whom it relies will suffer long-term negative consequences. Furthermore, if it is decided some time in the future to fix the problem, more pain will have to be endured. The leg may have to be re-broken. Other compensating conditions (e.g., back problems, etc.) may also have to be addressed.

Putting temporary conditions around a violated trust can, therefore, serve as a cast on a broken leg. While awkward and uncomfortable, they serve to enable the emotional consequences of a broken promise to heal. Doing so gives us the opportunity to re-build what had been lost. But doing so also has the opportunity to build an even stronger foundation of trust.

"How so? You ask.

When we are confronted with the need to start over with building trust, we are given the opportunity to deepen our understanding of several other abstract ideals that are essential to our efforts to achieve excellence.

Healing a broken relationship enables us to expand and extend the limits of our levels of acceptance, tolerance, forgiveness and humility of others and ourselves.

And, ultimately, it is qualities like these that will enable us to deal with the trust-busing termites that are a part of all relationships.

Week 29
Ditch Those Old Tapes

Illustrated by Bryant Fukutomi

Self-talk is a key factor determining true self-confidence—one characterized by humility and grace, a documented quality of successful leaders. Digging into the roots of self-unfulfilling self-talk will bring us face-to-face with a level of "touchy-feely stuff" not normally seen as acceptable coaching topics.

This stuff to which I am referring are internal tapes that have been recorded very early in our lives. Frustrated parents and teachers regularly implant messages that we carry into our adult lives. A repeated sharp voice and menacing finger when we spill a glass of milk: "How many times have I told you to be careful!?"

becomes encoded into the "I'm not worth very much!" file in our self-esteem program.

All that changes as we get older is the context. Any mistake gets treated as if it were "spilled milk." Only now the "sharp voices and menacing fingers" are our own, and they are playing out on the stage of our mind.

How many times have we heard or used the phrase: "He pushes my buttons!" That imagery is affirming a current event that has the power to activate a previously recorded internal tape. Once activated, the tape plays itself out as if the current precipitating event was the same as the original set of circumstances, including a replay of our own initial set of reactions.

Making up our minds to change the make-up of our minds, therefore, means we have to be willing to explore the historical roots of our responses to questions like:

» "How do your react when you've made a mistake?"
» "How do you celebrate and acknowledge your successes?"
» "What kinds of situations cause a knot in your stomach?"
» "What kinds of conversations are particularly difficult to have with your boss?"

Such explorations, while difficult to voice, can lead to important insights.

In my own case, for example, no achievement was ever "good enough." A 95 percent on an exam elicited the question, "What happened to the other 5 points?" A score of 100 percent often got the wry comment, "I guess it was a really easy test!"

Consequently, if I am not careful—very careful—that tape can negatively influence my current performance in several ways. I can inappropriately allow almost all of my energies in a training program, for example, to be drained away by the one or two people out of 100 who seem to not be "liking me."

I can end up ignoring, and not adding energies to, the 98 who are motivated to apply what we are learning. Needless to say, I've heard managers, and subordinates, complain of the same dynamics.

What can be done? How do we go about changing the makeup of our minds? Unfortunately, simply replacing negative statements with positive statements and affirmations—re-recording new content over the old tapes—is not likely to result in a long-term change.

If you've ever tried to talk someone else out of their negative self-talk, you've experienced this. They say something self-disparaging. You counter with something meant to be positive like; "Come on, you know that's not true!" or "Aren't you being overly hard on yourself!" If their tapes are deeply grooved, you'll either get a half-hearted shoulder shrug, or an immediate counter-argument: "Yeah, but you're my friend and you're biased" or "You're always looking at the half-full glass."

This ping-pong game will continue for a while. They will put themselves down and you will try to pull them up. But, pretty soon, you get tired of the game. You shrug your shoulders and quit trying to make them treat themselves better. Soon thereafter, a silent voice goes off in their head saying something like, "Boy, I must really be a loser. Even my best friend has stopped complimenting me!"

Score yet another victory for a self-unfulfilling prophesies.

Making up our minds to change the make-up of our minds will require a bold new approach, well beyond re-recording. Well beyond simply "thinking positively."

Week 30
How To Sabotage Yourself

Illustrated by Bryant Fukutomi

Imagine for a moment a significant other in your life, a spouse or best friend, who regularly chastised you with comments like the following:

"You're always making stupid mistakes!"

"When will you ever learn to plan ahead!"

"Boy was that a dumb comment!"

"You should know better than that!"

In reaction to this kind of verbal treatment (or perhaps we should say "mis-treatment") we can easily imagine a range of responses and reactions we might have.

Silent entries begin being made in that place in all of our minds and hearts where we keep track of emotional hurts. We begin to look for opportunities to get even, to balance the emotional books—to lash out, directly or with cutting

93

humor—by responding in (un) kind. Resentment builds, increasing the likelihood of blowing our cool.

When the verbal mistreatment gets to be more than we can handle, we will find a way to leave the relationship, to divorce ourselves from it. We might just up and quit. If, however, we can't do that, we can remain physically, but disassociate ourselves psychologically.

In other words, if we had a friend or significant other who treated us that way, we would tell them to "cut it out" or to change their tune. If these efforts failed, we'd cut them out. We'd disassociate ourselves from them. We'd stop considering them to be our best friend, a dear colleague. We'd stop living with them. We'd stop listening to them.

"Interesting psycho-babble," you may think. "But what has it got to do with leadership and creating excellence?"

Embedded in this dynamic may be the most powerful tool we have available to ourselves for the development of our leadership potential and personal excellence.

Need more proof? You can refer to a massive body of empirical research on cognitive emotive therapy, beginning with the landmark research by Albert Ellis.

Or you can more simply prove it to yourself. Make one small change in the statements above, and you will have a mere sampling of the kinds of dialogues many of us entertain in our minds regularly:

"I'm always making stupid mistakes!"

"When will I ever learn to plan ahead!"

"Boy was that a dumb comment I made in the meeting!"

"I should know better than that!"

In other words, many of us speak to ourselves in ways we would never tolerate from our best friend or a significant other. If we send ourselves negative messages like these with enough regularity, we will come to believe them. And, when we believe them, we will act in ways that make them come true.

Believing is the precursor to seeing.

As I have worked in intensive coaching relationships with senior executives, I have increasingly seen this self-unfulfilling prophecy in operation.

The scenario goes something like the following: The person calling me in describes my new potential coaching client as accomplished, well educated, experienced and successful. But a "certain something"—hard to put a finger on—seems to be missing.

My initial discussions with the coaching candidates uncover a comparable picture. They are competent at what they do. But they seem to be having a hard time embracing, with humility and grace, the fact that they are competent. For lurking just under the surface, their self-talk continues to undermine their confidence in who they are and what they do.

I stress this distinction for a very specific reason. Take a good look at the word confidence and you'll see that, in order to "get it," we have to be willing to "confide."

Consequently, coaching whose primary challenge is increasing confidence walks a very thin line between doing therapy, which is not the role of a coach, and creating an environment and a process that has the potential for the person being coached to experience "therapeutic learnings."

When we decide it's time to change the way we talk to our selves, we have to be prepared to confide to ourselves, and to our coach, a level and type of information not normally voiced aloud—and particularly not by "successful, competent senior executives who have been rewarded for their ability to suck it up and not let touchy-feely stuff get in their way."

Week 31
Be Your Own Best Friend

Illustrated by David Swann

Simply re-recording positive messages over old tapes won't change our self-talk. Counter arguments to the contrary—self-spoken or from a friend—"You are so good!" "You should look at your achievements!" "Stop beating up on your-self!"—are no more effective. Indeed, they can often be heard as yet another form of "chastisement," albeit delivered via a velvet glove.

So what is the bold new approach which is required if we are to be successful at making up our minds to change the make-up of our minds? To become capable of being more successful at the inside job of leadership self-development?

The answer lies in a paraphrased version of one of the Buddha's words of wisdom [the word hate was in the original]: "In this world, [self-deprecation] never dispelled [self-deprecation.] Only love dispels [self-deprecation.] This is the law, ancient and inexhaustible."

The implications of this 'inexhaustible law' are quite simple to articulate—and incredibly demanding to put into operation. In order to meaningfully change negative self-talk, in order to increase self-confidence, we must learn to do several things.

(1) First, we must be prepared to be fully present, to invest the time and energy to really hear out these internal voices. We must learn to be patient.

(2) Next we must learn to be understanding. To be able to paraphrase the essence of what is being voiced as a way to identify their negative expectations for what they are: old tapes versus current realities.

(3) Finally, we must learn how to empathize with the historical roots of these tapes, and the their recent costs and consequences. Not sympathize. Not take away the pain, the fear.

When we step back from this simple sounding short list, an important insight emerges. The steps being outlined are exactly those that we would hope to be able to take if we were approaching the person who was exhibiting negative self-talk as if they were our best friend.

In other words, the only way to successfully counter a self-unfulfilling prophecy over the long term is to befriend it. Not out run it! Not "override" it.

We need to learn how to be our own best friends.

Not because it is a nice 'touchy-feely' luxury. No, quite the contrary. Because the single most important quality in most studies of successful leaders is their ability to "care for others as human beings." And, we don't need Buddha to remind us that we must first care for ourselves as a precondition to caring for others.

But, to develop this ability to create and sustain increasing levels of self-confidence, we have to face an inevitable Catch-22—and there is always a Catch-22 in any human challenge of any substance. A coach may be necessary to start, especially a coach who is good friends with him or herself, and who is capable of exhibiting the patience, understanding, and empathy essential to being a good friend to their client.

Let me be very clear: I am not taking that position as a way of touting the value of good coaching in leadership development. I am stressing it for two reasons.

One, it is the very quality of our self-perception that needs sharpening and honing when our self-confidence is at stake. To try to do so alone would be akin to an optometrist grinding a new pair of lenses for their glasses, while wearing the old glasses that were giving him distorted vision in the first place!

Two, the process of having to reach out to someone else, to learn to trust them, to be willing to be vulnerable—to confide in them—involves challenges that give us the humility and grace to inculcate new tapes of lasting value—tapes that remind us "Only Gods are perfect," tapes that remind us that "Admitting a failing is not only not a sign of weakness, it is a sign of strength."

These are the tapes that help to strengthen our humility, our tolerance, and our acceptance of ourselves and of others, our self-confidence.

Leading by example and walking our talk are two frequently referred to challenges and pillars of leadership development.

Underlying both of them is the challenge of self-talk, of learning how to be our own best friends.

Week 32
Organizational Transformation:
Myths And Realities

A delayed flight recently gave me the opportunity to browse through an airport bookstore. I was interested in seeing what the buzzwords were being touted as the answers to "Everything you need to know about organizations and leadership to be successful." The ones that caught my attention were variations on a single theme: transformation.

If we are going to propel ourselves into the turbulent seas of ambiguity, which characterize the search for excellence, we need a much deeper understanding of what organizational transformation really entails. In particular, we need to be able to distinguish the challenges and dynamics associated with organizational transformation as distinct from large system organizational change. And, very importantly, we must be very clear on the personal implications for those who would presume to be transformational versus change leaders.

No single chapter can do justice to the importance and timeliness of these challenges. Consequently, the next four chapters will be devoted to this topic to give readers a deeper understanding and appreciation of a phenomenon essential to the never-ending search for organizational excellence.

Let us begin by dispelling some myths, by being clear as to what real organizational transformation and real organizational change are not.

A disappointing number of senior executives approach the challenges of transformation or change as if it were the equivalent of a magician's pulling a rabbit out of a hat. Typically, they will call in an outside consultant and, in effect, ask that person to wave a magic wand. "Schzam, abracadabra, transform my organization!" Of course, they do not use those exact words. Rather, they ask if it were possible to put together a two-hour session on transformation, preferably one deliverable over lunch so as not to take up too much valuable work time. And, oh, by the way, they may not personally be able to attend due to their busy schedule.

Neither transformation nor large system change are the result of a course, or even a series of courses, in isolation. They are not quick, painless, or "for them and not us/me." Organizations are, at their core, made up of individuals. Consequently, individual transformation and change are necessary preconditions to organizational transformation and change.

Furthermore, these processes are not done with "smoke and mirrors." While I may appear to look different when I am in the house of mirrors, my core being remains unchanged. The organizational equivalents of these dynamics are painfully clear these days. For example, massive amounts of energy and resources are invested in public relations, in the attempt to create an external positive image. These efforts rely on "spin doctors," professionals who can turn a sour lemon into sweet lemonade. They are skilled at taking a truth and packaging it to look more positive. Their brethren in the house of mirrors carry this approach to even more dishonest lengths. They cook up the books, creating false profits so they can line their own pockets. Tens of thousands of families, and their children's futures, become shattered when the undistorted truth is brought to light. Transformation is an inside-out job, not an outside-in game.

Finally, and perhaps most important, both the magician and house of mirrors approaches lack the integrity essential to any lasting transformation or change. And without integrity and the active heartfelt involvement of everyone, organizational transformations and large system changes efforts are more mythical than real.

In our next chapter, we will focus on differentiating large system change from transformation.

Week 33
A Crab By Any Other Name....

Illustrated by Dave Swann

The first chapter in this series, described two approaches to either organizational transformation or change—the Magician and House of Mirrors—that are more mythical than substantive. We shift our focus in this chapter to the dynamics of large system organizational change. Intense. Stressful. Essential. And not to be confused with the fundamental transformations organizations will have to undergo to stay on the path of excellence.

Nature provides us with a powerful set of images to help make this distinction. Let us begin with a crab whose normal life cycle contains multiple large "system changes." At various points, the crab finds itself having outgrown its shell. In other words, it must molt in order to be able to grow to its next natural stage of development. However, when it has successfully navigated this change process, it will still be a crab. Essentially the same as it was before. Bigger. Stronger. Meatier. But still a crab.

The first important factor to notice in this process is that it is the result of the crab's success. Had the crab "failed" since its last molting period—i.e., been eaten up by the competition or been unable to fend for itself—it would not be in a position to have to go through another round of growing pains.

So much of what is written and believed about organizational change has its roots in a defensive posture: "We have to change or we'll fail, we'll die." The crab or lobster reminds us that the motivation for needed change can be equally driven by the need to manage the consequences of success.

In my many years as a consultant, I have noticed how little attention is paid in organizations to the unique challenges presented by the need to manage success. There are a plethora of opportunities to take courses on problem solving or correcting mistakes. But I've never, in my experience, seen a formal management course on Success Management. And make no mistake about it; the skills and mindsets needed to manage success are not merely the opposite of those needed to solve problems. It would never dawn upon us, for example, to celebrate a problem or not try, at least, to learn from it so as not to repeat it. On the other hand, we also generally do a very poor of celebrating a success, and seldom take the time to analyze it so we can repeat it.

So, crustations remind us of two important qualities of the dynamics of large system organizational change. First, it can be motivated by an organization's natural cycles of growth. In contrast to the disappointment and potential pain associated with needing to manage an unanticipated abnormality, a failure, it can be the pleasant, normal result of having been successful.

However, simply because the change is motivated by natural and positive forces of success, does not mean the change will be without pain. Here again crustations provide an essential reminder. When a crab is managing and coping with its normal successes, when it sheds its existing hardened outer shell, it enters a period of intense vulnerability. Like a large organization that has been through a major growth spurt, in the period between shedding an old skin and developing a new one the crab is in a weakened state. Its natural predators know this and they will redouble their efforts to attack. Organizationally this can range from trying to pirate key employees who might be uncomfortable with the uncertainty that often accompanies such rapid change to hostile takeovers of those whose cash flow cannot keep up with their rapidly increasing appetites.

As a senior leader, ask yourself the following question: What specific steps do you take to protect your organization when it is going through the vulnerability associated with normal growing pains?

"Fine and good!" you say. "But what about when the changes are driven by the need to down-size to stay alive? When survival, and not success, is paramount?

We will address this important issue of the periodic need for a pruning in the next chapter.

Week 34
Born To Fly…Other
Transformations In Action

Illustrated by Bryant Fukutomi

You might want to be a bit more careful as you go about your daily life. Otherwise you may inadvertently bring an early end to one of nature's many transformations, one full of lessons for organizational leaders. For up ahead might be a very slow moving, currently earth bound, multi-legged creature we'd all recognize as a caterpillar. If this ponderous, relatively unattractive "seed of an idea" doesn't get prematurely "squashed," we may next see it safely ensconced in a protective cocoon, its home for the next phase of its transformation. "What can this miracle of nature teach us about organizational transformation?" you wonder.

One vitally important set of lessons has to do with the fact, that transformations have their own underlying rhythms and paces. We must be patient and humble as this pace unfolds. Imagine yourself watching the butterfly struggling, oh so very hard, to break free of its constraining walls. In a well-intentioned but misguided attempt be of help, you might reach out and make a little opening to help it along. And, in so doing, you may have inadvertently assured that the butterfly does not grow to its fullest potential. You may even have put in jeopardy of an early demise.

Why? Because it is in the very process of pushing itself out into the real world, where it must be able to cope and survive without the warmth and protection of its womb-like cocoon, that a butterfly develops the wing strength to soar.

When we work out on weights in the gym, we are using resistance to get stronger. Similarly, organizational resistance to a transformational idea or process is not, in and of itself, a bad thing. The challenge is turning this resistance, which, again, is a natural aspect of any major transformation, into a positive force. One that strengthens the organization's heart and soul for the journey that lies ahead. Indeed, looked at from this perspective, leaders should be suspicious of the total absence of any resistance.

But perhaps the greatest challenge that this natural and positive phenomenon of resistance carries, lies within a transformational leaders own heart and soul. We need only look to the one transformation that each and every one of us has personally experienced in our lives to prove this point—our own birth. Or, better yet, since we have no conscious memories of our own births, having been present when one of our own children was born.

There is a period during the final stages of this miracle of all miraculous transformations that the medical profession labels as 'transitional pain.' During this period, if the mother has chosen to be awake and un-medicated, the following scenario would be typical. On the one hand, mother and father are about to experience one of life's most joyous transformations—one they may have wanted, planned for, and prayed for. On the other hand, the mother is screaming and yelling blasphemous obscenities at her doctor, the nurses, and even her husband, her partner in creating this transformation.

There comes a point in many organizational transformations that brings with it similar dynamics. Even though there was excited consensus on the value of beginning the transformational journey. Even though there was equal enthusiasm as the emerging transformation began to take visible shape. When the actual time comes for the transformation to 'be born,' natural second thoughts should be expected. These will range from relatively simple questions like: "What did we get ourselves into?" to much more intense angry outbursts: "How could you lead us into such a painful place?!" The later are invariable aimed at the "father" or the "mother" of the idea.'

To be the leader of an organizational transformation requires the skill and attitude of a mid-wife, the ability to be with another's pain while being fundamentally helpless to do anything about it. Facing this pain is difficult. Consequently, many leaders during this period of transformation bury themselves in their offices behind mountains of computer printouts. Compassion, empathy, humility, and faith—not data—are what is needed at this time.

All organizational transformations, as we've noted in an earlier chapter, involve major organizational changes, but all organizational changes are not associated with transformations. As we shall see in the next and final chapter in this series, compassion, empathy, humility and faith are the building blocks for all meaningful personal transformations. And organizational transformations are, at their fundamental cores, personal transformations.

Week 35
Confiding Can Dispel Debilitating Fear

Illustrated by Jaime Ubongen

"Even a thought, even a possibility can shatter us and transform us." Friedrich Nietzshe

In the earlier chapters in this series, we have spoken of organizations as experiencing major changes or transformations. While convenient and typical, such depersonalizing terminology masks a very important truth. Organizations, at their core, are human 'beings.' Consequently, not until a critical mass of people individually experience a transformation will an observer notice that an organizational transformation has taken place. And the people leading this critical mass must be the organization's senior most leaders.

So, in this final chapter in the series, our focus shifts to the dynamics of major personal transformations and changes. The similarities noted will not, to re-emphasize, be accidental. They are a function of an organization's essential human nature. I will use myself as an example.

Some 15 years ago, I decided it was high time I learned how to swim so I could enjoy Hawaii's aquatic riches. It took enormous energy to overcome my resistance, my fear of looking stupid, and my embarrassment at being almost 50 years old and unable to swim. But I pushed myself to wander down to the YMCA and sat down with Henry Kamaka, a Hawaiian swimming legend in his own right, to figure out which would be the best class for me.

Much to my surprise, and chagrin, Henry also informed me he was <u>not</u> going to teach me how to swim. His primary job was to convince me [which he did] that, unless I chose to do so, I could not drown!

Floods of ego-related lessons are reflected thus far in this story for those who would be the leaders of organizations in the throes of a transformational pro-cess—the most central of which is that fear is our greatest enemy. In an organiza-tion such fear causes a 'hardening of the arteries'—people stop communicating openly and honestly. They begin to hold their breath. Confidence wanes. And the only way to regain confidence is to notice that it begins with the word 'con-fide.' Fear can only be dissipated by being spoken of and empathized with, not stuffed.

After successfully graduating, Henry invited me to take a lesson in lifesaving. I said "Sure!" Seconds after I put my hand under Henry's "drowning chin," Henry had both of us under the water.

As a consultant hoping to facilitate a transformation, the lesson was painfully clear: Until the key members of an organization—beginning with its lead-ers—surrender to the fact that they need help, the best that you can do is stay close by, continue to offer your assistance, and maintain faith that all will be OK. The hard part is to resist the temptation to be a 'savior' before they are ready to be saved.

As you review all the points above, you will, no doubt, be quite aware that suc-cessfully leading transformations has little, if anything to do with the "hard stuff"—budgets, pert charts, compute data, and the like. Quite the contrary! It is the "soft stuff"—humility, empathy, openness, faith, and the like—that will determine the success of a transformation.

Why? Because, organizations, at their core, are human 'beings.'"

All transformations begin with the power of one.

Week 36
Sale On, Sale On, Salesman

Illustrated by Dave Swann

Recently, a long-standing client for whom I had done considerable leadership development work asked me to design a training module for the company's sales people. The specific concern was that many staff seemed to be losing sight of the organization's fundamental premise. Namely, building win-win customer relationships was the key to successful long-term sales.

Don't let your natural "Ho hum, what else is new?" immediate response lead you to stop reading. Like you, I knew that premise was true before they asked me for a "new program." I noticed, however, that in putting together this new program about an old truth, I was continuing to reach for bits and pieces from the previous work I'd done on leadership development. And then it hit me.

Every manager and leader in an organization that enjoys any long-term degree of success at what they do does so because they have learned how to be a good salesperson.

Their "customers" are their colleagues. Their "products" are their ideas, proposals and plans to keep the organization on the path to excellence.

It is their ability as sellers to form and maintain win-win relationships with these "customers" that results in loyalty and commitment, the cement that holds the organization together.

A few examples on the direct parallels will suffice. It is well documented that sellers who simply describe their product's or service's features and advantages over their competition's are generally unsuccessful. On the other hand, sellers who can make direct and clear benefit statements to their prospective buyers are very frequently rewarded with the sale.

"Given what you said about needing X, elements Y and Z our product will be of specific relevance to you." A benefit statement, in other words, links directly to a buyer's need.

And how do sellers get potential buyers to voice their own needs? The sellers exhibit what I call their "pull skills." By giving their full attention, they create an environment where the potential buyer feels invited to think aloud about what they need and why. By asking open-ended non-leading questions, and actively demonstrating that they understand what is being said, they demonstrate that they have listened and heard. Then, and only then, are they in a position, to use their "push skills" to make a benefit statement.

"Nice theoretical idea," you think, "but the parallel breaks down because real customers have a choice to buy or not." And you are right, in part. Employees who report to you cannot decide not to "buy your proposals." But having identified their specific needs can still be of value in helping you to explain why they can't be met this time. Commitment and loyalty can be preserved when you don't have to ram the product down the customer's throat with no logical explanation.

And then, of course, there are those cases when the customer for your idea is your own manager, who has a choice to buy it or not.

So my suggestion is simple. The next time you find someone resisting buying an idea you've been trying to sell, take a wander over to your own sales department. See if you can get your No.1 salesperson to have a cup of coffee. Tell her that you would benefit from any advice on how better to package and sell your idea. Specifically ask how to deal with buyer resistance.

My bet is that if you listen really carefully, what you will hear is that the top salesperson exhibits a high degree of very skillful behavioral flexibility. The best ones have learned how to adjust behavior to the needs of a specific buyer, and across different buyers who also have different needs. Not necessarily product-related needs but most certainly relationship-related needs, i.e., how they need to be treated to feel that you are trying to create a win-win relationship.

This relationship is directly parallel to current research on effective leaders. They, too, just like successful salespeople, have the behavioral flexibility and sensitivity to vary their approaches to meet their colleagues' needs.

Finally, I am acutely aware that whether or not you have bought this argument, whether or not you see it of benefit is completely a matter of whether or not you feel a personal need to become a better leader.

Week 37
Take Time To Smell The Roses

Illustrated by Bryant Fukutomi

Every organization claims, "Our people are our most important asset." Yet, the strategy of continued cost cutting to drive up short-term corporate profits may be having severe negative long-term consequences that we seem to be ignoring. The scenario goes something like the following:

You feel really grateful and relieved to have survived the last few rounds of down-sizing. Many of your work colleagues were not as fortunate. While they got pretty good severance packages, and most have found some kind of new jobs, many had to uproot their families and move to new locations. The whole process left emotional scars on them and their families.

So when you boss says, "I need those reports ASAP!" lunch goes by the way-side, or some less-than-healthful fast food is gulped down at desk-side.

If it's a really big job, and the "I need this…" message comes late Friday after-noon, the family will likely hear, yet again, an explanation for your weekend absence. While you may resent these erosions into the quality of your life, you also know that "Silence may be the better part of valor."

Indeed, I've heard many employees admit that there is an unspoken new rule these days. No complaining about being over-worked. There is a long line of peo-ple who would love to have your job.

The cost and consequences data are unequivocal. Since 1973, the average American is working 142 hours more a year. We are the only major industrialized country in the world "whose citizens are not entitled to a vacation by law." The average American takes 13 vacations days a year, half as many as the average South Korean or Japanese worker—countries by no means noted for their lack of productivity!

And, here's what may be the real killer—literally and figuratively. Of Amer-ica's workers entitled to a vacation, 26 percent never take it. This, in spite of the fact that medical research clearly documents that the consequences of not "taking time to smell the roses:" include heart attacks, stokes, high blood pressure and other stress-related illnesses.

The Japanese who don't take vacations call it "karoshi"—literally "death from overwork." Estimates put the karoshi figures in Japan at a conservative 10,000 people a year.

In other words, this pattern of self-sacrificial behavior comes at no small price. By allowing this pattern to continue, we are enduring steadily increasing health risks and a steadily eroding quality of life, for our families and ourselves.

And we cannot even, albeit foolishly, justify this pattern as resulting in increased workplace productivity. It is hard to imagine how people living poor-quality lives can actually contribute over the long-term to significant quality improvement at work.

Working harder does not equate with working smarter. Indeed, working smarter may actually require the physical, emotional, and spiritual re-energizing and rejuvenation a vacation is intended to provide.

But the real costs may be more subtle. When employees begin to feel impris-oned by their jobs, a pattern of resentment and denial begins to build up. Bodies continue to show up for work, but hearts, minds and souls are increasingly with-held. The result, as we have noted in other chapters, is that up to 50 percent of a broad spectrum of America's middle management and general work force is just "hanging around and marking time" until they can retire.

This means that more pressure to produce will continue to fall on a shrinking minority workforce of committed loyal employees.

In the face of this mounting pressure, either the ranks of the "hangers around" will grow, or the medical consequences experienced by those who skip lunches and vacations will become exacerbated.

Ignoring quality of life while striving to enhance quality at work may prove to be lose-lose.

Week 38
Power Use It Carefully

Illustrated by Bryant Fukutomi

Power, we've been reminded, corrupts and absolute power corrupts absolutely. But power itself is not the corruptive force. Power is neutral until two or more human beings decide to convert it into influence. Abusive uses of power, therefore, are reflections of abusive relationships between people, of conscious choices.

Strong language or ivory tower stuff, you think? Let us explore just two of the ways we consciously collude to allow power to be "used wrongly or improperly"—Webster's definition of abuse.

The first has to do with the tyranny of large numbers. Consider the following universally replicated laboratory research findings: When confronted with two vertical lines—A, which is 6 inches in length, and B, which is 4 inches in length—thousands of diverse and representative individual subjects, viewing the two lines alone in a room, report being absolutely certain that A is the longer line.

Now imagine other comparable subjects seated at the corner of a round table occupied by four other 'naïve' subjects, just like themselves—they think. Unbeknownst to the one in the hot seat, of course, each of these paid stooges has been instructed to select B as the longer line.

Video cameras focused on the hot seat capture a variety of quite funny gestures. Puzzled looks. Scratching heads. Removal and cleaning of glasses. Leaning forward for a clearer view. What is not the least bit funny is the fact that an average of 30 percent of those in the hot seat yield to the group pressure and report that B is the longer line. I'll leave it to your imagination to abstract from these "ivory tower" conditions to the boardroom conditions, where the stakes and consequences are absolutely opposite.

As long as we are now at the boardroom table, let's add to the pressure to conform—to "group think"—the "small" factor of positional power because the seat at the head of the table is occupied by the boss. If you cringed even a bit at the "length of the line" research, be sure you're sitting when you look up an article entitled "Studies in Social Obedience" by Stanley Milgram.

Imagine the following scene: A presumed academic expert on learning wearing a doctor's white coat is in a room at a prestigious university—Yale, Harvard, Pennsylvania, Columbia, to name four where the research was originally conducted. You are seated next to an electronic generator you absolutely believe can transfer 450 volts of electricity in 15 volt increments to a subject in another room you absolutely believe is hooked to your machine.

The results? Absolutely 100 percent of those reading this article are certain they would NOT be blindly influenced by a combination of expert, referent, and positional power to flick all 30 switches (30 times 15 equals 450 volts) to deliver the fake electricity to the subject. None of us reading this article are among the 50 percent who actually did!

So, given that nothing gets accomplished without the exercise of power and influence, what can we do to guard against groupthink? Here are three "logical suggestions."

(1) Ask people just for the sake of argument to argue for the position opposite to the one they support.

(2) Really listen to the minority voice vs. the perfunctory, "OK, speak your piece…and then we'll move on." If it's a truly new idea, then the majority will not see it immediately.

(3) Be sure feedback is immediate, face-to-face, and specific. If you have the positional power, be very suspicious if you've not gotten any constructive criticism lately.

But, of course, the bottom line when it comes to power and influence has absolutely nothing to do with logic. It has absolutely everything to do with having the courage to speak the truth to power.

Because when we don't, we are colluding in ensuring that power becomes abusive.

Week 39
Plug Into Power

Illustrated by Bryant Fukutomi

The gap between the plethora of good ideas many employees have for how to improve their organizations, and the number of these ideas which actually get implemented, is maintained by a self-imposed shackle of powerlessness.

"If I ever suggested XXX to my boss, I could kiss my career goodbye."

"I'm just one voice, what can I do!"

"They won't listen to any new ideas."

Without denying the fact that others will resist change, seldom does the "powerless one" step back and ask themselves the question: "Am I tapping into a source of power that will connect with the other person and influence her/him to join with me in converting my idea into action?" This question will lead to five sub-questions and issues.

(1) Do I have any expertise that can be brought to bear? Is there anything about my formal education, my documented experience, publications, hard data, and the like that might fuel my attempts at influence?

If the answer is "Yes." and the issue is one that is open to logical debate, then Expert Power may be one of the influence ingredients you can call upon as you formulate an influence strategy.

(2) Are there any powers I can get delegated to me? When Sean Connery knelt before the Queen of England and she touched his shoulder with her ceremonial sword, she gave him a healthy dose of Referent Power. When and if it was useful, he and others could refer to him as Sir Sean Connery. People who particularly respected British Royalty would attribute a higher level of esteem and power to Connery as a result.

References from respected others that accompany a job application are meant to serve a similar effect. As is networking with other like-minded colleagues who may have an easier time selling your idea than you might. As is "reference" to the fact that "the boss suggested I come and ask you to help me on this project." The abusive use of this source of power is the well-known "name dropping game" that characterizes highly political organizational environments.

(3) Do I have direct control over things that matter—currencies of value—to the person I need to influence?

If so, and if I'm prepared to use them as negotiating chips, then what is traditionally called Reward and Punishment Power may become an element of your influence strategy. The key word, of course, is the word "and." Because if you're not careful, playing a trump card can result in either winning the trick or getting over-trumped.

(4) This brings us to the issue of Positional Power. The obvious facts are that some people have it and others don't, and that some people have more of it than others. The less openly acknowledged facts about this source of power are two: One, it is "nothing personal." It wouldn't matter whether you, I, or anyone else reading this chapter were named the CEO of Corporation X, we'd inherit certain positional powers. And, two, when used in its most abusive forms—kicking butt, taking names—it will at best, yield grudging compliance, and require virtually no skills at all!

I am not saying that being a CEO requires no skills. Quite the contrary. Specifically, because of the power the position carries with it, being a boss requires an extraordinary combination of both intellectual and emotional skills. These are personal sources of power. They are not bestowed or inherited from a written job description. They are earned. They can be learned. They are what underlie any degrees of the personal Expert Power and Referent Power we may enjoy. The rubber meets the road in the power game when we add the element of Positional Power into this mix.

No one would argue that being a good subordinate is hard work and it can be risky. But few would see that being a good boss is hard work and it's risky.

"Why risky?" you wonder? Because the power to abuse position works two ways. The danger of the boss over-using it is no less than the danger of the extent to which others blindly bow to positional power.

To emphasize the point we made in an earlier chapter, the bridge between a source of power and its potential for influence is a relationship between two or more people. The vehicles, which transform power into influence, are the relationships between human beings making similar conscious choices. Abusive uses of power, therefore, are reflections of abusive relationships between people.

Week 40
Juggling Act

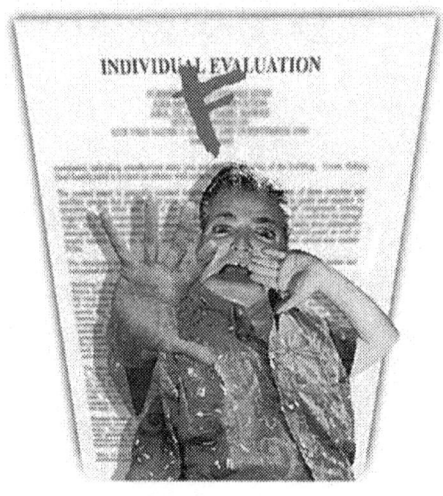

Illustrated by Kip Aoki

Intuitively, every manager understands the need to manage the fear of failure. For, if employees are griped by this "disease", they will be very hesitant to exhibit a diversity of behaviors essential to any organization's growth and development. Anything that involves some risk, like trying out a new idea, a new skill, or even bringing some bad news to the boss, will either often be approached with undue hesitancy or avoided entirely. A lose-lose is the result.

The organization loses the short-term opportunity for a potential improvement. And progress not perfection is our lot in life. But the long-term consequence is perhaps even more important. Because the employee has suffered yet another lose of self-confidence, the probability of the future and continued risk-taking essential to growth is reduced.

Recently, however a colleague, very astutely noted the relative inattention to another one of management's greatest fear-related challenges, the fear of success.

The roots of both fears go deep. Think back for a moment to your childhood. Did your parents ever "get on your case" if you made a simple mistake? If you tried something new and took a long time to get it right…or didn't get it right the first time? If you only got average or below average grades in school? If you talked back to one of them? These kinds of early experiences plant the seeds of the fear of failure.

But, how can anyone fear success you wonder. When I brought home a 95 on a school exam, my father wanted to know what happened to the other 5 points! If I got a 100 on the exam, he wondered aloud if perhaps the exam wasn't too easy.

What are frightening similar about both of these fears are their consequences. They leave the person gripped in them feeling: "What difference does it make? If I try and don't make it, I'm going to get some form of punishment. From chewed out to maybe worse."

Now let's look at the other side. If I try my hardest and do make it, I may also fear I'm going to get some punishment. Only, in this case, it wouldn't be getting yelled at. Instead, it will be having to deal with such 'rewards' as, for example, having next years budget reduced and cut back by the amount I managed to save in this year's budget.

I may have to deal with even more unrealistic expectations for next months work load because my team did a super-human job of meeting this month's goals with a staff reduced by downsizing. This one is particularly insidious these days.

More than one of my senior management-coaching clients has told me, with much chagrin—since it violates their own sense of integrity—how hard it is to really try their best. Because the reward of a job incredibly well done is another unrealistic mountain of work

This entire dynamic reminds me of a booth at a carnival, the one where you had a rifle and were shooting at a bear. Every time your shot hit home, the bear would be sent off in the opposite direction. When an organization is "whipping" its people around in a similar manner, with the way in which it manages both failure and success, standing still in the middle of the road has to be safer. Don't get me wrong. There is nothing wrong with the middle of the road. It is, however, not the path taken by those in search of excellence.

This behooves every manager who would profess to be trying to lead a team in search of excellence to take a good look in the mirror and ask some hard questions. How does my own behavior encourage my people to deal with me face-to-face when there is a problem, particularly when it is my own behavior may be a part of the problem? When mistakes are made—and they will,—do I create an environment where the focus is on learning or blaming? When we achieve a success, do we take some quality time to really celebrate or do I say: "You're expected to succeed. Now let's get back to work."

As French poet and playwright Alfred de Musset has warned us. "Perfectionism does not exist; to understand this is the triumph of human intelligence; to expect it is the most dangerous kind of madness."

Week 41
Conflict

Illustrated by Kip Aoki

Remember your days as a student in the chemistry lab? Part of any exam involved being given a vial of an unknown liquid. In order to determine its contents, the vial would have to be carefully heated over a flaming Bunsen burner. If left under the heat too long, the vial might crack, spilling the contents. If removed from the burner prematurely, the necessary catalytic reaction might not occur. A delicate hand and sensitive eye were needed to pass the test.

Conflict presents a comparable test. We are all familiar with one edge of the sword of conflict. Sweaty palms and racing hearts serve as a constant reminder. If we lack the sensitivity and skills needed to stay on the edge to manage conflicts, well, blood, in some form, may be shed—from resentments or broken relationships.

On the other edge of the blade of conflict lies the creativity; the unexplored, unconsidered and typically highly divergent ideas essential to those in search of organizational excellence. As Simon London put it in the Financial Times, "Major disagreements among corporate executives can be a waste of time and money and cause damage to working relationships, but they also can be a healthy way of sharing (and creating) new ideas if managed effectively." Several things will help a management team have healthy conflict.

While the normal emotions stirred in any significant difference of opinion are highly personal, it is vital that in the heat of the moment, there be no personal attributions. "You're being as stubborn as a mule!" will only serve to fan the flames of defensiveness." "Can you summarize what parts, if any, of what I've said that you agree with?" will be potentially more productive for several reasons.

First off, it will serve to facilitate more active listening to counteract the normal tendency in the heat of battle to selectively focus on differences vs. similarities. Second, if any similarities in positions can be identified, the potential for discovering a common alternative will exist. And the identification of common goals is key to conflict resolution. Third, taken together, these two factors also can increase the number of options on the table. Debates centered on only one or two options are considerably more likely to turn into hardened positions.

Humor is also a _potential_ tool. I underscore the word potential however to remind us that humor can also be a two edged-sword. It can lighten the mood for everyone, as well as cut someone off at the knees. Humor must be employed with sensitivity and integrity. Its intention must be sincerely positive—to oil a point of friction—vs. being used as a masked form of hostility.

Perhaps the most difficult obstacle in the way of a "good fight" has to do with how the team, and its leader handle to issue of positional power. Heavy-handed leaders are able to create the illusion of collaborative conflict resolution. All of the important differences get buried under a false consensus around a decision that, in reality, reflects the boss's preference. Laissez-faire leaders do no better. The leadership vacuum they create only exacerbates conflict.

The ideal is one of balance. The leader and the team members have the boss be part of the group, vs. apart from the group, while not denying his or her power position.

But, of course, teams and leaders who have learned how to balance this reality day-in and day-out have already developed the kind of healthy team culture that enables them to have good fights when they are called for.

Week 42
Unfair Treatment Bites

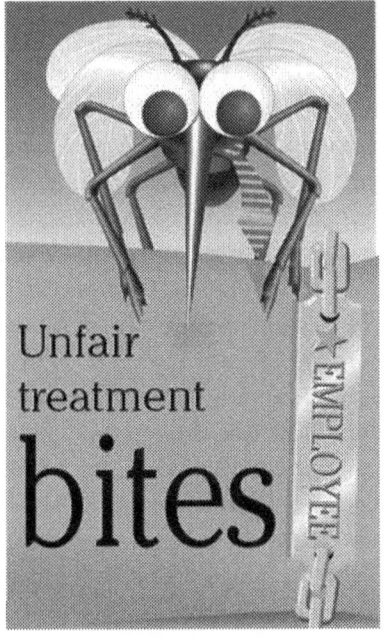

Illustrated by Bryant Fukutomi

As I was preparing our outdoor grill to barbecue some chicken wings recently, I found myself having to stop every few seconds to swat yet another mosquito who was seeking to feed upon me. In addition to this being an irritant, I was also a bit confused.

I'd purposefully put our grill under our carport, far away from the foliage in our backyard where these pesky critters lived, to avoid exactly this problem. A little nosing around the area uncovered the cause: a garbage can lid had been left open-side up and gathered a pool of stagnate water. A nirvana for all the mosquitoes in my backyard had become a hell for me.

A recent study conducted by the Watson Wyatt Worldwide Consulting Group strongly suggests a comparable situation is brewing with respect to employee performance appraisal and incentive programs. For some employees, these systems are a nirvana, motivating them to proactively seek places and opportunities to sink their teeth into important organizational problems.

They remain loyal, often shunning opportunities to fly off to what may appear to better opportunities. And, when they buzz with excitement to their friends, they are actually helping the organization recruit fresh new blood as eager and motivated as they are themselves.

So what, if you'll pardon the pun, is the fly in the ointment, you wonder?

The key lies in the word "some." The organization's high performers appreciate what these systems do for them, claiming they improve performance reviews and pay decisions. What "bugs" them are that the daily routines of the organization's poorer performers are not affected. The poorer performers are allowed to stagnate and subsequently breed discontent among others who are trying to improve.

In other words, while star performers—the ones who are invariably enthusiastically buzzing around—are often praised, their poorer performing colleagues—the ones who are invariably laying low to attract minimal attention—are seldom, if ever, confronted.

A combination, these star performers note, of goals that are often non-specific, and feedback that is seldom direct and honest, is debilitating.

I am not suggesting that attention paid to star performers be at all reduced. Rather, I am emphasizing the need to take steps to lighten the load being carried by star performers because there are un-addressed situations of employees who are not carrying their fair share. Employees who are permitted to not pull their own weight, to stagnate and not improve will—like a mosquito—suck needed blood from others.

Most encouraging about the Watson Wyatt Worldwide Consulting Group study results was the extent to which employees were eager for companies to revamp their accountability standard and systems in order to further motivate the high performers, and at the same time address the poorer performers.

Employee performance systems that support organizational excellence sit on three legs of a stool:

(1) Clear, specific, measurable goals and performance targets, tied to à priori consequences: If X, then Y.

(2) Frequent direct, face-to-face (none of this anonymous 360-degree stuff) honest feedback. [See The ABCs of Effective Feedback: A Guide For Caring Professionals for more on this topic.]

(3) The systems-and the managerial courage and commitment to use them, that deliver on the à priori consequences above.

Ultimately, the situation will arise where a poorer performer cannot be motivated or trained, to improve. Like the dead branches on a tree, if that wood is not pruned, it will continue to stymie growth. Not confronting poor performers does not make the problem go away. Quite the opposite. Such avoidance will, invariably, sap the spirit from even the most motivated employees.

Take a good hard look at your employee performance and incentives systems. Do they remind you of the flowing and regenerative Red Sea? Are they supporting and growing an organization full of mostly live coral and active beautiful fish?

Or do they remind you of the stagnant Dead Sea? Are they supporting and harboring an organization full of mostly crusty old salt and deep mud?

Have your performance appraisal and incentive systems become more of an exercise in bureaucratic minutia?

Have they, in the words of an anonymous observer, become like "any sufficiently advanced bureaucracy indistinguishable from molasses?"

Week 43
Keep On Smiling

Illustrated by David Swann

A comment during a training session on styles of leadership by a senior executive working for a large Federal Government agency got me thinking about the infectious nature of our moods. I had noticed during the session that he generally had a broad smile on his face, was optimistic about the future, and was upbeat and open-minded about learning and trying new things.

It came as little surprise to me when the group was identifying the qualities they would be seeking in the people they would define as their "ideal leaders"—the people they'd be most willing to follow—a constellation of behaviors I label as "inspiring" was his No. 1 rank. He was a man, in other words, who tried to "walk his talk."

What got me thinking, however, was not the fact of his integrity—inspiring as that was—but the following dialogue. When I commented that, in my observation, his own behavior seemed to mirror the "inspire" style, he, and the others in the group, all nodded in agreement. (His ability to "graciously accept" such praise was another of his leadership qualities.)

When I asked, "What kind of feedback do you get regularly from your colleagues about your enthusiasm?" he breathed a deep sigh and for an instant, the twinkle in his eyes paled. "Generally none."

Then he paused and, after another sigh, added, "If I get any feedback, it is more likely to be little barbs like: 'So are you ever going to share what ever it is you are smoking!' or 'Somebody must have gotten another bonus!'"

Several very poignant reminders emerged from this interchange.

For so many people, time at work can become a prison sentence—a non-fulfilling experience that consumes the major part of their waking hours five to six days a week. Smiles, if they occur, are plastic and forced. Learning and trying new things are shunned under the rationale of "old dogs being unable to learn new tricks." They end up counting the days until their "parole." Their dreams focus on retirement and the hope of a golden parachute. And it is the rare person who can prevent bringing these same feelings home to their own families.

"How was work today?" gets in return a short "Same old same old!"

One has to wonder what young children are learning about what they can expect from their own careers from listening in to those short, repetitive exchanges.

This smiling 'inspired' colleague, on the other hand is—and wants to be—fully present in the moment. His mind and his heart are unclouded by negativity. Consequently, he thirsts to absorb, understand, and appreciate all the good things going on around him now.

When listening to others ideas, he hears them as opportunities for making things even better versus putting up immediate barriers: "Don't rock the boat!" "We've done it this way for years!" His family often comments that it is hard to get him to stop talking enthusiastically about work when he gets home.

But perhaps the most poignant reminders were embedded in the feedback barbs he related. First, the psychology fueling these reactions is quite simple: projective jealousy. In other words, his colleagues, in their hearts, would like to be able to manifest comparable levels of enthusiasm.

But for their own often deeply rooted reasons, this natural human desire gets turned into throwing cold water on the spark of a burning ember versus adding ones own energies to making it glow even brighter. (I stress "natural human desire" because it is hard to believe the gift of the miracle of life had an asterisk note in fine print to the effect that birth carried a lifetime "prison sentence.")

Second, the existence of these barbs—subtle and obtuse as they may be, including the total absence of any positive feedback, any acknowledgment of the enthusiasm being exhibited—brings into stark relief one of leadership's greatest challenges. An old Sufi saying put it best: "I never taught anyone archery who at some point did not aim their arrows at my back."

True leaders, in other words have no choice but to strive to "walk their talk" and not succumb to others efforts to talk them out of their walk.

The best that true leaders can hope for is that others will feel inspired to walk alongside them.

Ultimately, it is followers who decide whether leadership is contagious...or not.

Week 44
It's Good To Monkey Around With The Status Quo

Illustrated by Kip Aoki

You don't have to be a rocket scientist to know that innovative new ideas are the lifeblood of any organization. In today's rapidly changing competitive business world, if you're not steadily moving ahead, you are, in fact, falling behind. It won't be long before your competitors leave you in the dust. However, it also doesn't take a rocket scientist to observe the numerous obstacles organizations put in the way of getting the very innovative new ideas they need.

Think about it for a second. How many times recently have you heard someone [or even yourself!] say, in response to the suggestion of a new and innovation idea, any of the following: "We don't do things that way around here." "We tried something like that a while back and it didn't fly." "That's a really interesting

145

idea but you'll first have to satisfy Policy X, Y, and Z before we can even consider it."

If you've worked in a large organization (which, of course includes government) you've heard more than your share of these statements, and a plethora more like them. The all reflect a simple truth about how organizational policies begin and get perpetrated that, as the story below points out, even monkeys can understand.

Start with a cage containing five monkeys. Inside the cage, hang a banana on a string and place a set of stairs under it. Before long, a monkey will go to the stairs and start to climb towards the banana. As soon as he touches the stairs, spray all of the other monkeys with cold water.

After a while, another monkey makes an attempt to get the banana with the same result—all the other monkeys are sprayed with cold water. Pretty soon, when another monkey tries to climb the stars, the other monkeys will try to prevent it.

Now, put away the cold water. Remove one monkey from the cage and replace it with a new one. (Even monkeys experience turnover!) The new monkey sees the banana and wants to climb the stairs. To her surprise and horror, all of the other monkeys attack her. After a second attempt and attack, she knows that if she tries to climb the stairs, she'll be assaulted.

Now, remove another of the original five monkeys and replace it with a new one. The newcomer goes straight to the stairs and is attacked. (The previous newcomer takes part in this 'hazing' with enthusiasm!)

Continue this 'turnover' process (after all, new blood is a supposed good!) and watch as all the newcomers get the same treatment from their teammates (most of whom are not really all that sure why they were not permitted to climb the stairs in the first place or even why they are making life equally difficult for the newest monkey.)

Now, here is the real kicker. After replacing all of the original monkeys, none of the remaining monkeys have ever personally been sprayed with cold water. Nevertheless, no monkey ever again approaches the stairs to try for the banana. Why? Because as far as they know, "That's the way it's always been done around here."

So, if your organization seems not to be getting the variety and number of truly new and innovative ideas it needs to stay ahead of the competition, here's a few simple questions you might want to ask yourself.

* When is the last time you did a thorough and rigorously honest assessment of all your organization's policies and procedures to see which ones have become out-dated?

* In what subtle (and not so subtle) ways do people's new and different ideas get 'doused' by you and or your colleagues?

* When you do bring some new blood on board, how long does it take for those people to look and act just like everyone else?

Why are these questions so vital? Because when it comes to human behavior in organizations, it doesn't take a rocket scientist to know the power of "monkey see, monkey do."

Week 45
Leadership Qualities

Illustrated by Dave Swann

The largest and most diverse investigation ever conducted in the United Kingdom ("Stamp of Greatness", by Beverly Alimo-Metcalfe and John Alban-Metcalfe 26 June, 2003, Health Services Journal) produced the most un-startling revelation. "Showing a genuine concern for people" was found to be the "single most important indicator of transformational leadership", predicting fully "60 percent of a person's final overall leadership score."

Why un-startling? Do we really need exhaustive, extensive, repeated and expensive research studies to prove a point common sense has taught us for ages? What goes around comes around. Organizations that treat their people well are rewarded for their efforts by employees who work hard and remain loyal to warrant the return on investment. Reciprocity is one of our most fundamental human natures, positive or negative.

The second thing we must note very carefully is that we are not talking about just 'being nice.' There are, in my experience, a whole ranges of behaviors that I can exhibit that will result in a person concluding that I am concerned about them. These include behaviors that we would normally see as fitting into a category we might call being empathic; but these are not the only behaviors we experience as reflective of a concern for us. A small sampling of the many others my own leadership research has uncovered in the past three decades would include paying careful attention when a person is speaking, caring enough to be honest and direct about my praise and constructive criticisms; and being humble enough to admit and apologize for my own mistakes.

In other words, concern means different things to different people under different circumstances.

The second key word is genuine. This element of transformational leadership demands that we be very self-aware. And self-awareness, as yet another massive body of research tells us, is the key to emotional intelligence—EQ in contrast to IQ—which distinguishes average leaders from the best.

Being genuine asks much of us. What we say has to be honest, has to come from the heart. Scheming by figuring out what you can say to make a person think you are concerned, when you really don't' care, is being manipulative. Most people see through such shams quickly, even though they seldom let you know they do. And if you really believe you can con your employees in this manner, you ought to be worried. For who wants to put the success of their organization in the hands of people who are so easily fooled?

So theoretically, becoming more of a transformational leader is as simple as ABC, as increasing your awareness of your behavior and its consequences.

(1) *Awareness*. Ask a person to tell you what specific behaviors they need to experience from you for them to conclude you are genuinely concerned about them.

(2) *Behavior*. Make a genuine effort to regularly exhibit those behaviors, and if need be, get a coach to help you learn how to do so.

(3) *Consequences*. Monitor the consequences of your behavior by periodically asking for feedback on how well you are doing, and, based on this added awareness, adjust your behavior accordingly to effect a more positive consequence.

Easy to say but hard to do. But that's why there are so few really transformational leaders—because enacting this simple dynamic cycle is, first and foremost, an act of self-transformation.

Week 46
Wisdom: That 'Something Extra' Of Leadership

Illustrated by David Swann

During my career, I have come across a vast body of research and writing on the issue of leadership. Is it born vs. made? If made, what are the building blocks? How do we impart these building blocks to aspiring leaders? Indeed, I have partaken in many a leadership development program myself, both as a participant and a teacher. Recently, I was reviewing the videotape a CEO coaching client sent me of a senior executive meeting he'd conducted, as a prelude to helping him to continue to develop his leadership skills.

I'd known from the first meeting we had that there was something extra-ordinary about his leadership style, but I never been able to pin it down. To be sure, he had an above average IQ. His schools smarts were matched by his street smarts; he came up through the ranks, so he knew what it meant to work in the trenches. His EQ, his emotional intelligence, and its resulting interpersonal sensitivity and skills were equally well developed.

And then, there it was in black and white on the playback screen before my very eyes. His extraordinary quality was staring me in the face. It was shouting out for me to notice it. What was I seeing? What was I hearing?

What I was hearing was a full 30 seconds of total group silence! What I was seeing was no nervous fidgeting of papers. No anxiously darting eyes.

Like most extraordinary qualities, however, I'd missed his because I was focused on looking for something I expected to see instead of just seeing what was happening. I'd forgotten a related lesson my father had taught me decades ago about spotting feeding fish. The trick was to not focus on looking for the movement of fish, for what I wanted to see, for what was going on "out there." Rather, the challenge was to look for what wasn't supposed to be there, for what was going on inside and underneath what was going on out there, like ripples going against the wave pattern, dimples on the surface of the water, colors sharply contrasting with those around them.

This new observation was high on my agenda of topics to discuss with him at our subsequent session. It seems that, early in his career, he had learned that when faced with a particularly difficult decision, both he and his executive teammates seemed to exhibit a specific array of group dynamics. Interruptions and over-talking increased in frequency. The normally more introverted and quiet of his colleagues leaned further back, away from the table, lest they somehow get caught in the periodic fusillades of verbal crossfire. Eye movements became more rapid as people tried to catch glimpses of others' nonverbal in hopes of identifying potential supporters or dissidents to the decision they knew was correct—theirs.

This CEO had learned that there are times when a group needs what no amount of intelligence, intellectual or emotional, or sophisticated leadership training can ever be expected to provide. There are times when wisdom is needed. And wisdom, like looking for feeding fish, comes from looking inside. Wisdom cannot be trained before the fact. It has to be uncovered and emerge.

So the next time you are your team are struggling to come to consensus on a difficulty decision, consider following this CEO's extraordinary quality. Ask everyone to just be quiet for a moment. Suggest that they go *inside* and see if they can identify what they know, in their hearts, is the right thing to do. What decision will truly serve the greater organizational collective good in its efforts to care for or about its clients, customers, or patients?

You may well be surprised at how quickly a true consensus is identified.

Silence may not be golden but it is often the path to it.

Week 47
Yin And Yang Of Leadership

Illustrated by Kip Aoki

In her book "The Chalice and the Blade: Our History and Our Future," Riane Eisler reminds us that our brains are designed to continuously root out and incorporate ways we can control, subdue and master our life's many challenges.

This "dominator model"—fueled as it is by our IQs—is absolutely essential to leadership competencies having to do with problem solving, strategic planning and the like.

However, successful leadership, as we are increasingly being willing to accept, is fueled by much more that just IQs, more than cognitive abilities. The single most influential factor causing high-potential, high-IQ young leaders to become derailed is their inability to form and maintain successful interpersonal relationships.

The key elements of a "partnership model" are respect, openness, cooperation and harmony. These qualities are what fuel our EQs—our emotional intelligence quotient. And this form of intelligence is not housed in the mind. It is housed in the heart.

Efforts aimed at leadership development, if they are going to be successful, must therefore be two-pronged. They will require a "yes" and not an "either-or" mind-set.

Let us examine some the challenges this involves. Think for a moment about the typical imagery we use when cognitive learning—when increasing or using our IQs—is the issue. We "cram" or "force feed" for an exam. We "pour" over documents. We "brain storm" ideas. We "attack" and try to "master" a problem.

See the pattern? We try to "yang" it into submission.

And there is absolutely nothing wrong or inappropriate about this—when IQ is what we are striving to develop, access or apply. However, when EQ is what we are striving to develop, applying, these same strategies will not work and will reduce the probability that the needed strategies become available.

If we attempt to "attack," "storm," or try to "master" our hearts, we will only succeed in closing them down, in making their doorways thicker. When this happens, we say a person has become "thick-skinned," "cold-hearted" or, worse yet, "heartless."

Leaders will often <u>unintentionally</u> manifest this feeling of "heartlessness" (or more accurately a lack of feeling) to others. I stress unintentionally because I am not speaking of those who get their kicks out of being emotional or verbal bullies. I am speaking of leaders who think they are doing the "right thing" by, for example, "steeling themselves" before they have to tell someone they've been fired; of leaders who jump right to stressing the facts of "generous severance packages" without allowing "down-sized" employees to grieve; to leaders who seem to have forgotten that being a human being, with both a mind and a heart, came before being a stoic professional.

In order for the heart to develop and release the respect, openness, cooperation, and harmony that fuel the "partnership model"—our EQs—we are confronted with an inevitable Catch 22. We must "yin" the heart into respecting us, trusting us, opening up to us and co-operating with us. Feelings can't be "crammed" into the heart. The heart has to open itself to them.

EQ-related skills—self-awareness, sensitivity, empathy—cannot be fully developed by cognitive means only. In the same way, by analogy, we cannot spiritually learn to ice skate.

Take a good hard look at your own leadership development efforts, for yourself personally and for your entire organization. How much time and energy is being invested in yang versus yin? Are dominator-oriented development strategies (reading, lectures, case analyses, PowerPoint displays) being used to help people secure IQ yang outcomes which are learned from the outside in?

Are partnership-oriented development strategies (coaching, experiential exercises, personal reflection, real-life relationships) being used in an attempt to acquire EQ yin-related outcomes which are facilitated from the inside out?

Don't be surprised if you discover a severe imbalance, if you find you and your organization's leadership development efforts are "over yang'ed and under yin'ned."

Or if you find that brain-related strategies of learning have been confused with heart-related needs for facilitation.

You won't be alone.

Week 48
What's Love Got To Do With It?

Illustrated by Kip Aoki

I watch my neighbor across the street in awe. When he is working on his lawn, he is meticulous, systematic, and totally absorbed. No short cuts. No looking at his watch every few minutes to see if it's quitting time. No supervisors looking over his shoulders checking on his quality.

I don't know what he's like at his regular job, at his career. But I'd bet my bottom dollar that he, at the very best, is no more motivated. In all likelihood, he exhibits considerably less of a "labor of love" attitude at work. And, it is in understanding what causes that difference, and closing the gap between how many people approach their avocations versus their vocations, that you are betting your organization's bottom dollars.

Tim Sanders, a senior executive at Yahoo not only understands the dynamic described above, he had the courage in a recent *Fast Company* article (February 2002) to even label it such: "The most powerful force in business is love."

Imagine that. In a rough-and-tumble, dog-eat-dog, nice-guys-finish last world of barracudas and sharks, where even the phrase "touchy-feely" is spoken with a tinge of disdain, we have a very senior executive in a very public (not to mention successful) company not only willing to use the soft "L" word, but to relate it to the very hard bottom line.

As if that wasn't enough, the "selfless promotion of the growth of others"—the definition of love Sanders has embraced from Milton Mayeroff's brilliant book, "*On* Caring—not only, as we will show shortly, serves the organization's bottom line, it is also self-serving.

It is a win-win-win. Why three wins? Because when you, as a leader, help others to become all they can be, you are helping them to scale the well-known Maslow hierarchy. You are propelling them toward self-actualization.

When as a result of, and in response to your love, a person becomes the very best that they can be, your organization has to benefit, and you also grow as a direct result yourself. You have taken a step toward becoming more of the very best person you can be. Altruism has nothing to do with it!

How does the organization benefit? Two examples should suffice. If more of your people felt that coming to work was an opportunity for a days "labor of love," how do you think that might affect turnover? Time spent talking stink about the company or supervisor? Sickness days? Grievances filed? Doing those "little bits extra" that are not a part of people's job descriptions but, when added up, make a big difference?

Those are the easy bottom-line-related indicators. More subtle but no less important is the well documented—and commonsensical—correlation between self-confidence, self-actualization, and creativity. Simply put, you will get your best ideas from people who believe their bosses sincerely want them to become the best they can become.

Not sure? Ask yourself how many Ms. or Mr. *Average Employees*—you know the ones; invisible, quiet, nothing special—have you seen become non-stop fountains of creative ideas when doing volunteer work? The difference is that they are made to feel important. Valued. Needed. Not bad synonyms for the "L" word!

Okay, so how can you as a manager demonstrate that you care? It's actually as simple as ABC.

A.   You increase your **A**wareness by asking a person what specific behavior they need for you to exhibit for them to feel cared for by you.

B.   You do whatever you need to do to learn to exhibit those specific **B**ehaviors.

C.   You periodically seek to adjust your awareness by seeking feedback on the **C**onsequences of your behavior.

By following those three simple principles, which are out-lined in my book "Having It Both Ways: The ABCs of Win-Win Relationships," available from www.amazon.com, you will quickly begin to see "what love's got to do with it"—regardless of whether "it" is a business or a personal relationship.

Week 49
Inquiry Or Inquisition?

Illustration by Bryant Fukutomi

I never cease to marvel at what can be learned simply by opening a dictionary. Today's "Ah ha!" experience was discovering that the words inquiry and inquisition are so close alphabetically that they sit one above the other. But in terms of their meaning, and the implications of those meanings for effective leadership and organizational excellence that's where their similarity ends.

An inquiry, we are reminded, is "the seeking or request for truth, information or knowledge." An inquisition on the other hand is "characterized by a lack of regard for individual rights, prejudice on the part of the examiner, and harsh, prolonged, difficult questioning...sometimes even resulting in 'recklessly cruel punishments.'"

I introduce these two definitions for two reasons. One, organizations are increasingly coming to recognize the vital importance of creating and sustaining a culture of learning versus blaming. And, two, they are—in my experience—still not helping employees learn how to become willing collaborative partners in a process of inquiry versus fearful avoiders of what feel like inquisitions.

Let's look at some of the more typical cues that an inquisition is in the making and how to more effectively manage them. Questions whose content focus is "Who?" or "Why?" will create problems on several counts. The latter invites a "because" response replete with rationalizations. The former invites "passing the buck."

These dysfunctional consequences will be particularly likely if the music in the tone of voice and non-verbal body language that come along with the words are not very carefully chosen. You can prove this to yourself right now.

Try to imagine that something important has not gone according to plan. Feel the natural and understandable frustration of the event. See yourself in your mind's eye asking "Why?" or "Who?" Can you hear a slightly raised tone of voice? Can you see the second finger on your dominant hand pointing or shaking a bit?

All of these will contribute to defensiveness, to less information and knowledge being shared, and maybe even to less truth being spoken.

While the heat of the moment will make it a challenge, focusing on "What?" and "How?" are much more likely to contribute to the needed inquiry. The reason for this lies in the behavioral interdependence inherent and inevitable in all systems.

The old '60s saying put it: "If you're not part of the solution, you're a part of the problem." In this case, because of the interdependent nature of human systems, everyone involved has made some contribution to the problem. Therefore everyone owns some responsibility and accountability for seeking and contributing to both the learning and the solution.

The leader has a unique responsibility and opportunity to set the tone for the collaborative non-judgmental environment needed. She or he does so by taking the lead in making "I" statements:

» "From where I sit, this is what I see has happened…"

» "I can see how I may have contributed to this situation by…"

As each participant shares their story of what has happened and how, the focus must be kept on non-judgmental attentive understanding—on inquiry. Not selective listening and debating in order to try to poke holes in someone's story—inquisition.

When leaders and group members both learn how to exhibit these kinds of behaviors, a quite remarkable thing happens: Very often, the underlying problem becomes patently obvious to everyone. It emerges in the areas identified as the differences between each person's story of what has happened and how…from their particular perspective.

And, to paraphrase our '60s axiom, because we were all part of the problem, we can now turn our attention to collaboratively being partners in the solution.

Is it worthwhile investing in this kind of behavioral training?

The choice is quite simple. Organizations that conduct inquisitions versus inquiries are less able to learn, adapt and grow. Like dinosaurs, they risk either obsolescence.

The difference between inquiry and inquisition may be one thin line in the dictionary, but when it comes to organizational excellence, it is the bottom line.

Week 50
Meetings: Can't Kill 'Em

Illustrated by David Swann

Among the many "love-hate" relationships that we experience in life, meetings would rank at the top of many people's lists. I thought I'd heard all the standard clichés and snide remarks but a new one caught my attention: "Meetings are places where someone takes minutes but everyone wastes hours."

So what I'd like to do in this article is first offer a few simple questions, which will take only a minute to explore, but might save everyone from feeling that they've wasted yet another hour. And second, ask you to consider an even harder question that might lead you to an even deeper understanding of what leads people to roll their eyes in resignation at yet the thought of another meeting that will "keep them from their real work."

Question One: What does your agenda tell people?

Take a good look at the last meeting agenda you sent out. Does it just list topics/times? Discuss Project X (10 minutes). Discuss Issue Y (15 minutes).

Or does it list clear outcomes and processes? Here are a few examples:

» Inform everyone about the status of Project X.

"Provide consultative input to Person A on Issue Y.

"Agree, together, on what to do about Issue Z.

The difference between the two agendas looks small but it can be huge. In the first case, there is no specificity to what is meant by "discuss." There is no outcome that is made clear.

In the second case, we see three very different types of discussions, each leading to a different outcome. Each, as we shall see below, requiring different behaviors for attendees to be successfully achieved.

Question Two: Do attendees understand their specific roles in contributing to the achievement of each of the agenda items?

Everyone's behavior, including the formal leader's, must be aligned with the particular agenda item. When being informed about the status of Project X, my job as a member is to

» Listen carefully.

"Ask questions for clarification.

» Demonstrate that I understand what is being said.

My job is not to argue or debate. When being consulted before the fact of a decision, my job as a member is to be able to exhibit the above behavior above AND argue as cogently and clearly for my suggestions and ideas as I can.

As the person receiving this consultative input, my job would be gate keeping—keeping everyone talking to me vs. arguing with each other.

Why no arguing? Because the only place where differences need to be ironed out is during that part of the meeting when a consensus decision must be made. During this part of the meeting debate will be essential, as will listening carefully, asking questions for clarification and demonstrating understanding. Note that as the agenda moves from informing to consulting to deciding, the behaviors members must exhibit are cumulative and require more skill.

Then there are the "harder questions!"

The harder question has several dimensions. One has to do with whether or not the meeting was real or make-believe. Was there so much political behind-the-scenes stuff going on before the meeting that all the real issues got taken care of then? If so—and it is frightful how often this is so—the apparent meeting is really just a re-run of an old movie. So the hard question one is: "Was the meeting really necessary in the first place?"

During the meeting itself, are there "sacred cows?" Are there issues that everyone knows are important but will not raise because someone—usually the boss—gets really upset when they are? As a consequence of these sacred cows, enormous energy is wasted dancing around vs. dealing with issues head-on.

Hard question two is: "Assuming a meeting is necessary, is the culture of the meeting safe enough for people to speak their minds so they can come to a meeting of the minds?"

So, what do you do if your meetings are really necessary in the first place, and the meetings' agenda goals and members' behavioral roles are crystal clear, and it still feels like they're not working?

Then you have one final hard question to ask: "Is it worth a few hours of your time to do an in-depth assessment—to put this complicated piece of human equipment up on the rack to see what is causing you to waste precious hours of your most valuable asset?"

If not, then your meetings will continue to be a place where "someone takes minutes but everyone wastes hours."

Week 51
Take Stock At Year End: A New
New Year's Resolution

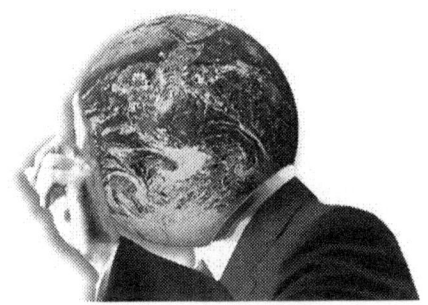

Illustrated by Bryant Fukutomi

[Authors note: This particular piece was written as the turning of a New Year approached.]

I have thoroughly enjoyed the opportunity to be able to share with my thoughts about organizational excellence with you. I have been enriched by the thoughts and ideas many of you have shared in return. As we move toward the close of yet another year in the business we share in common—living on and working in Earth, Inc.—I thought it might be stimulating to frame this article as a hypothetical report to all of us as stockholders.

I felt some hesitancy, in the context of what follows, using the imagery of a CEO. I do so with only the utmost respect for each readers' perception of their own Higher Power.

Best wishes to one and all for a happy, healthy, and peaceful new year.

TO:	All Employees
FROM:	CEO
SUBJECT:	Report to Stockholders: Earth, Inc.

As we move through the early stages of our third millennium, I feel a need to take stock of Earth, Inc.'s business history and future. Our fundamental mission, albeit under increasingly severe threat and attack, is unchanged. That is, to evolve into an even more loving, beautiful and creative planet, a perfect reflection of my cosmic being. Earth, fire, water, and air remain the essential elements needed to support our business. Please keep in mind, these elements are finite, both in supply and quality.

The bottom line will forever be our people, some 6 billion strong. None of our conglomerate subsidiary organizations—families, churches, schools, industries, and governments, to name a few—can survive, let alone succeed, without them. Without its people, every organization becomes like Earth, Inc. was "in the beginning…without form, and void."

Let me digress a moment. I've become aware recently that many of you wish that Adam's and Eve's employment dates had been simultaneous. I confess, quite frankly, the reason is that Mother Nature and I hadn't yet conceived of twins. I hope you'll forgive me. I really did not mean to imply a preference between the genders.

As you all know, a clear division of authority and responsibility is vital to the success of any business. I will outline what I perceive to be my areas of authority and responsibility. As your CEO, I will continue to provide the gift of life and the assets that will allow you to live it to the fullest. Like a snowflake—one of my favorite inventions, by the way—each of your human forms is unique in its expression, yet all are given these gifts in common.

Three of these assets are tangible:

1. Bodies to support your physical natures;

2. Hearts to support your emotional natures;

3. The most powerful of personal computers, brains to support your creative natures.

These three tangible assets are finite and are susceptible to abuse, just as are our basic business elements, which I mentioned earlier. Add to these assets those which are intangible, infinite and, perhaps, the most important: your souls, which support your spiritual natures.

I have given you dominion over the fish of the sea, and over the fowl of the air, and over every living thing that moveth upon the earth. Therefore, in the business of living, you are all CEO's. As such, you are individually and collectively responsible for the consequences of your choices. The truth is that by the choices you make today, you will—in fact and by design—determine the forecast for tomorrow.

"The policies that guide human beings in aligning their behavior with our reason for being—our fundamental mission of creating love—are vital to the success of our business. I will be available to help as I have always been. While the queue is often times long, my door is always open. And if you have an emergency, you may refer to our first policy manual, the Ten Commandments. Or, you need only invite me through prayer to join with your souls in guiding your bodies, hearts and minds to distinguish right from wrong.

In fact, I strongly recommend heartfelt silent prayer and meditation. If you look into your own hearts and minds deeply enough, you will recognize that you already know what is right. Oftentimes, my help simply affirms your own faith and courage.

Any business that fails to take a regular inventory risks going broke. An inventory is a twofold process: First you must find the facts, and then you must face them. I can hardly overemphasize this latter step. Always keep in mind that your objective is to discover the truth about the stock in trade. If you should discover damaged or non-salable goods, get rid of them promptly and without regret.

To be successful, business owners cannot fool themselves about fundamental values. Values are your guides, so choose them wisely. At the risk of being repetitive, let me remind you that as employees of Earth, Inc.—in the business of living—you are all CEO's.

As Earth, Inc. moves forward, I will continue to serve as your collective CEO. However, if you should choose to follow leadership elsewhere, as you have often threatened to do in the past, I can only pray for the serenity to accept the things I cannot change, the courage to change the things I can, and the wisdom to know the difference. Sound familiar?

I love you, one and all, and I remain your faithful servant.

Week 52
"What's It All About, Alfie?"

Illustrated by Jaime Ubongen

Our first year of weekly "curbside consultations" has come to a close. Each reader will no doubt, have their own list of "takeaways. Points that stick with them. Parts they feel motivated to return to and reread. Ideas they will share with others and try to implement themselves. My own effort to reflect once more on "What's management and leadership about?" led me back to my trusty dictionary. A Webster's originally published over a century ago.

Management I discovered used to be primarily defined around the concept of "careful treatment." Sure, there are other definitions that revolve around "skillful manipulation" and the like. Alongside this "careful treatment" definition was a quote: "A prince of great aspiring thoughts; in the main, a *manager* of his treasures."

So my own reaction to the question: "What's it all about, Alfie?" revolve around a series of questions I continue to ask myself. They are questions I hope you will continue to ask yourself and your colleagues. They are framed in the context of truths most everyone accepts as common sense. Truths we seem to have difficulty putting into common practice.

Virtually every management and leadership "best seller" in the last several decades* has merely provided a variation on a theme articulated in the 'first management' text ever written, the Bible. When as a manager or a leader you are "Doing onto others." can you in your heart say it reflects "How you would have them do unto you?" What makes it so difficult for us to embrace the fact that treating ourselves and others 'care-fully' is an essential element of good management and leadership? What do we fear we will lose by acting toward one another in a fully caring manner?

There are, as the saying goes, no atheists in foxholes. In other words, in our deepest often unspoken cores, the over-whelming majority of us believe in a power greater than ourselves. As human beings we are [as far as we know!] the most the most advanced species this power has created. One must wonder, therefore, how our day-to-day behavior might look different if we accepted the responsibility and accountability we have of being "a manager of *His* treasures?" The 'treasures' we claim publicly are our 'most important assets'. What behaviors of our own would we strive to change? What behavior's we observe in others would we no longer passively accept as 'business as usual?'

People who, through no fault of their own, suffer from split personalities live very stressful dis-eased lives. Without any conscious intention to do so, they also cause stress and dis-ease for those around them. Keep this thought in mind the next time you hear yourself or a colleague use the phrase; "Let's behave '*professionally*.'" What is it that has led us to separate being a holistic human being from being a professional? What is it that 'professionals' are "not supposed" to think and feel and say that we grant as a right of human beings? What are the costs and consequences of this unwritten form of organizational pressure that tells us getting ahead means having to wear two different faces: one as a professional at work, and one as a person outside of work?

So let's try, in the jargon of the day, to drive to the bottom line. Let's assume that perspectives on "What management and leadership are all about?" will have a different slant depending on age, gender, race, nationality, industry, education, experience, hierarchical rank, learning styles, and even the nature of one's breast feeding toilet training! At the end of the day, no matter how we cut it, however, the bottom line involves human beings relating to human beings.

Great advances are being made in the creation of robots which can help, for example, people who suffer from autism. However, as Edward R. Murrow once noted, complex machines only increase with speed the ultimate challenge of one human being having to communicate with another. To be sure, equal strides are being made to make use of robots on organizational assembly line-like tasks.

The day may well come when "employee ranks" are filled with robots. If and when this becomes true, management and leadership, as we know it, would be irrelevant issues. Management and leadership 'training' would become a sophisticated exercise in programming 'superior robots'. 'Employee development' would be done with a can of WD-40 etc.

However, for the time being, when the "it" involves the management and leadership of human beings versus robots, the answer to the question "What's it all about, Alfie?" is straightforward.

Quality management and leadership are all about quality relationships.

*Including my own, I must say. See the short bibliography in the Appendix.

Appendix

My Pulse Is Not What It Used To Be: The Leadership Challenges in Health Care, Rubin, Irwin M. Ph.D. and Fernandez, C. Raymond M.D., (Kingsham Press, 2003) available through www.amazon.com

The ABCs of Effective Feedback: A Guide for Caring Professionals, Rubin, Irwin M. Ph.D. and Campbell, Thomas J. M.D., (Jossey-Bass Publishers, 1997) available through www.wiley.com

Having It Both Ways: The ABCs of Win-Win Relationships, Rubin, Irwin M. Ph.D. and Campbell, M.D., (Kingsham Press, 2003) available through www.amazon.com

Caring Matters: Everyday Tales for Healing Organisations, Fraser, Sarah W. Ph.D., Wilson, Tim, Rubin, Irwin M. Ph.D., (Kingsham Press, 2005) available through www.amazon.co.uk

Dying for Compassion, Rubin, Irwin M. Ph.D. and Boden, T.W., (Kingsham Press, 2005) available through www.amazon.com

Temenos Inc.
temenos@lava.net
www.temenosinc.com

978-0-595-41202-0
0-595-41202-5

www.ingramcontent.com/pod-product-compliance
Lightning Source LLC
Chambersburg PA
CBHW020411290526
45785CB00002B/505